Coffee

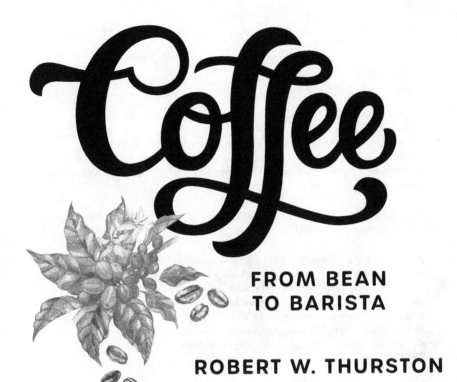

Coffee

FROM BEAN TO BARISTA

ROBERT W. THURSTON

ROWMAN & LITTLEFIELD
Lanham • Boulder • New York • London

Rowman & Littlefield
Bloomsbury Publishing Inc, 1385 Broadway, New York, NY 10018, USA
Bloomsbury Publishing Plc, 50 Bedford Square, London, WC1B 3DP, UK
Bloomsbury Publishing Ireland, 29 Earlsfort Terrace, Dublin 2, D02 AY28, Ireland
www.rowman.com

British Library Cataloguing in Publication Information Available

Library of Congress Cataloging-in-Publication Data

Names: Thurston, Robert W., author.
Title: Coffee : from bean to barista / Robert W. Thurston.
Description: Lanham, Maryland : Rowman & Littlefield, [2018] | Includes
  bibliographical references and index.
Identifiers: LCCN 2018012460 (print) | LCCN 2018015579 (ebook) |
  ISBN 9781538108086 (cloth) | ISBN 9798881808914 (paperback) |
  ISBN 9781538108093 (electronic)
Subjects: LCSH: Coffee. | Coffee industry.
Classification: LCC SB269 (ebook) | LCC SB269 .T54 2018 (print) | DDC
  338.1/7373—dc23
LC record available at https://lccn.loc.gov/2018012460

For product safety related questions contact productsafety@bloomsbury.com.

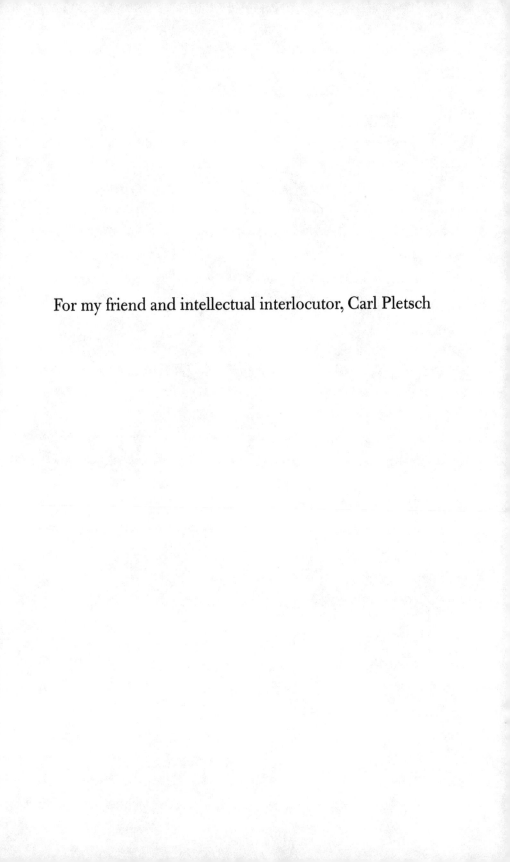

For my friend and intellectual interlocutor, Carl Pletsch

Contents

Acknowledgments

So many debts to so many people! I can hardly name them all here, but I especially want to thank and note the generosity of Professor Tonya Kuhl, UC Davis; Salvador Loucel and Hanna Neuschwander, WCR; Manuel and Christian Castaneda, Marcala, Honduras; Benjamin Paz Muñoz; Lowell Powell; and Carlos Robert Pineda and Orieta Pinto of IHCAFE. I thank Chen Zhao for guiding me around Yunnan, China.

Emily Puro, editor of *Roast Magazine*, and her corps of readers for an article I wrote about recent research on coffee all helped get my thoughts about the science of the plant into decent shape.

For a while, I had a personal microbiologist, Professor Luis Actis of Miami University. He even made house calls! Thanks, Luis, for going over genetic markers and much more with me.

Thanks also to Susan McEachern of Rowman & Littlefield, who had faith that I would write this book and get it to her on time. Maybe someday we will meet; I'll buy the coffee.

My wife, Margaret Ziolkowski, has patiently listened to me talk about coffee for years. I have asked her to sip or actually drink many coffees and have always been eager to hear her opinions. And I have made those requests to a dedicated tea drinker! She read through the manuscript of this book and made many stylistic and substantial comments. OK, some of that was payback for my listening to her talk about Russian rivers and dams around the world.

ACKNOWLEDGMENTS

My daughter Lara has been wonderful about running the Oxford Coffee Company and about engaging in a long give-and-take with me about how to roast beans and how to make drinks. She has been helpful to me in ways she may not realize. I very much appreciate her skill in working on the photos and other illustrations for this book.

1

Introduction

Anyone with the good fortune to visit a coffee farm has the opportunity to take in a host of powerful impressions. First is often striking beauty in a near-perfect climate. Sometimes you can look out over ridges stretching into the distance, down a steep and green valley, or even to the ocean. The air is clean and the temperature doesn't usually get above the low 80s Fahrenheit (28–29 degrees Celsius), although the sun can be fierce. On a farm that is treating the earth well, birds are abundant, flowers line the roads, and in the right season, the coffee trees bear voluminous white blossoms.

My own favorite moment on a coffee farm was in Nicaragua years ago. I was in a group hiking up a steep trail, the lush foliage almost closing off the sky above. I felt thirsty but had no water with me. When I looked down, I noticed oranges lying on the ground. As I picked one up and peeled and ate it, a flock of small, bright green parakeets took off from the trees. I had to stop for a minute just to try to absorb the intensity of the experience.

Yet near that farm, as has happened so often and will happen again in coffee country, tragedy also marked the landscape. Nicaragua was torn apart in the 1980s by fighting between the leftist Sandinistas and the Contras, conservatives backed by the United States. People had been killed in the area around where I stood. Although the land was peaceful by the time I arrived decades later, several villagers who had lived nearby had starved in recent years, when the price they got for their coffee was abysmally low. Traditional life and values had seriously eroded there and elsewhere in Nicaragua, mimicking the slow destruction of the wooden houses by termites; at night the people watched awful Spanish-language comedy shows broadcast from Miami, and drank.

A similar story played out in Colombia in the 1980s and '90s. In that struggle, too, leftist guerrillas fought the government, again supported by the United States, until a truce was signed in 2016. The worst episodes of all, in a civil war that also followed the basic left-right script, devastated Guatemala for thirty years. Rebels, but above all the army, killed many peasants. Entire villages of Mayan Indians were wiped out.

The history of coffee has seen many dark times. Almost all coffee in Brazil, and much of the coffee in Cuba, was picked by slaves for more than a century until they were emancipated in 1888 and 1886, respectively. The Dutch forced their colonial subjects in what is now Indonesia to deliver coffee without pay from the late seventeenth into the twentieth century. Day-to-day unfree labor—for example, indigenous people forced to harvest coffee—was all too common in coffee lands until very recently. Reports from Brazil speak even today of forced labor on the farms, especially of young men essentially held prisoner by landowners and local police, who confiscate the workers' documents and money.

As against all that, and even considering the negative impact of global warming, many bright spots characterize the coffee industry. Its total value—all the money paid around the world for coffee beans or drinks, and for wages and other direct costs—remains open to educated guesses, but somewhere above $100 million annually is surely correct, and the figure is growing. Coffee is not, incidentally, the second most valuable commodity traded around the world. It is the most important tropical agricultural product, but it is way behind even other crops like wheat. If huge profits for coffee are out there—for instance, at Starbucks or the J. M. Smucker Company, which sells Folgers coffee—farmers may receive a pittance for their efforts, or nothing at all, as their beans may be ruined in cultivation, harvesting, or processing. Fifty million coffee farmers is a nice round estimate; they grow the plants on more than 10 million hectares, or 27.4 million acres. Many of the smallest producers live on the edge of disaster. Chapter 2 examines what is happening in coffee cultivation, especially its current challenges and the work to deal with them.

Coffee production has soared in the past fifty years, so that today the world has three times as much coffee as half a century ago. But almost all of that increase has occurred in only two countries, Brazil and Vietnam, and the

Coffee terrain varies greatly. The top picture is relatively flat land on the Conquista farm, Minas Gerais State, Brazil. The second picture is from central Costa Rica. Large machinery can be run over flat land; where the hills are steep, coffee must be picked by hand.
Photos by Robert Thurston

largest share of the growth in supply has been in a rough-tasting species, *Coffea canephora, var. robusta*. Just about everyone in the business refers to that plant simply as robusta.

Various sources say that worldwide, people consume 500 billion cups of coffee per year.[1] Who knows? That's also a pleasantly round number. And just what does a cup mean, anyway? Chapter 3 will discuss that not-so-minor question, along with roasting, brewing, and coffee consumption by country. Just under two-thirds of American adults drink coffee every day, according to a 2015 poll—a figure that has hardly changed since 1999.[2] If intake is not rising in the United States, the International Coffee Organization (ICO) still projects a 25 percent increase in global demand for coffee from 2015 to 2020. That seems possible, but such a rise depends on continuing economic improvement from Latin America through Asia and Africa, as well as on attracting more people to drink coffee. Recently the growth in consumption has been largely in new markets for the drink, especially in Eastern Europe, Russia, and China.

Workers returning to their housing on a large Brazilian farm, one with good working conditions. The satellite dishes on the houses indicate that the standard of living is fairly high. To the right, coffee trees are arranged in neat rows in the iron-rich soil.
Photo by Robert Thurston

Like many kinds of agriculture, coffee farming has become mostly an older person's job. The average age of a coffee farmer in Colombia is 56, in Africa 60. This is not unusual; the average age of all Japanese farmers is about 66. So one of the challenges facing coffee is how to keep or draw younger people to agriculture. Villages must become more attractive places to live. To my mind, the Nicaraguan countryside is already preferable to the crowded capital, Managua. Perhaps nongovernmental organizations (NGOs) might work on cable TV for all and good transportation for an occasional visit to a city.

Climate change threatens the supply of both robusta and *Coffea arabica*, the milder, more flavorful beans, around the world. Spanish is the second language of coffee, and we can trace the spread of *broca*, the coffee berry borer, to every producing country and to higher altitudes. *La roya*, coffee leaf rust, reduced the Central American crop by 40 percent in some countries in 2014. Temperatures in several growing areas of Colombia have risen on average by a few degrees C (4–5 degrees F) in the past several years, causing significant problems with flowering. Each flower lost on a tree means that coffee berries, which contain the seeds (beans to us), will not grow at that point on a branch. Rainfall may also be inadequate or too heavy as the climate changes.

But the bad news is offset to some extent, or so we in the coffee industry hope, by good news in other respects. Research on breeding arabica plants that are better able to withstand pests, disease, and drought is ongoing in virtually every coffee-producing country. Many efforts to crossbreed arabica with robusta are under way. So far, the results are hardier plants, but ones whose beans don't taste as good as those from the more fragile, more "pure" arabica. Yet that result will undoubtedly change. Meanwhile, farmers are taking various steps to reduce the impact of global warming.

Work on the genetic structure of coffee, which aids in hybridization, has been in progress for decades. Scientists use genetic markers to try to determine which ones are linked to disease and pest resistance and which are related to taste in the cup. From the lab to hybrids in the fields and back to the lab to start over— this is painstaking work.

Research on the coffee plant and hybridization is in a race against time, not only as the climate changes but as coffee's enemies rapidly mutate. Falling behind in this race may someday bring the industry to embrace genetically modified (GMO) coffee. Although none is for sale now, and the researchers I have spoken to say they are not working on it, someone somewhere surely is. Robusta's DNA, approximately half as long as arabica's, was sequenced in France in 2014. In January 2017, scientists at the University of California, Davis, sequenced the genome of arabica. Mapping the genes opens the door wider to GMO coffee, although such tinkering with robusta first began in 1999. But above all, scientists are looking for genetic markers; knowing them greatly speeds up the work of breeding new plants. Chapter 2 explores this process. Meanwhile, organic coffee farming, which forbids GMO and most—although not all—synthetic sprays and fertilizers, continues to grow in popularity among consumers. Chapter 2 also looks into the pros and cons of organic coffee farming.

Neither the worries nor the progress should affect the enchanting experience of drinking a fine cup of coffee. In the consuming countries and now in numerous producing ones too, having a respectable cup of coffee can provide solid benefits to the farmers, the earth, and the distribution of wealth around the world. If you are ingesting coffee drinks from beans already ground and sold in a plastic tub for $3.00 a pound—dollars per pound is still the international way of pricing coffee—you are not doing much for coffee farmers. But if you move up to coffee grown carefully, roasted to reveal its inherent quality, and made into a drink carefully in a conscientious shop—in a phrase, specialty coffee—you are helping the coffee world. The liquor (to use the industry term for the coffee in any drink) made in such a meticulous way will put you as a consumer at the forefront of social justice and environmental progress.

For me, drinking really good coffee, with no milk, sugar, or flavoring to alter the taste that comes from the beans themselves, can be a sublime experience. Even if I don't see the oranges and the parrots in my mind, I do sometimes conjure up images of the farms I've visited. And above all, I can lose myself a little as flavor notes emerge, as my tongue senses the degree of sparkle and body in the liquid, and as a long and complex finish lingers in my mouth and mind.

Allow me to invent a word: *organolepsy*, like narcolepsy but a whole lot better. *Organoleptic*, a term that does exist, refers to the sensory qualities of just about anything, hopefully of anything good. To get a full experience with wine, you first pour it and smell it. You swirl the whites briefly and the reds more vigorously to see if they have legs, taste a bit, think about colors and flavors and how much body the drink has, and then sip. The finish of good wine is long and impressive. You clink glasses to add another dimension, sound. Altogether, good wine provides an organoleptic—pleasing to the senses—treat. Fine coffee, taken black, can do all that too, except you may seem a little weird if you clink cups. If you like a hazelnut latte made with decaf and almond milk, whipped cream on top, I don't mind. Just don't expect a transcendent experience. Chapter 3 discusses how roasting brings out the flavors in coffee and how the most careful shops make it, along with a little history of the plant's spread around the world and a discussion of what "sophistication" means.

Whatever you sense in a cup of coffee, it is now abundantly clear that the drink is generally good, perhaps excellent, for personal health. Chapter 4 explores the latest findings on this subject and explores coffee's impact over the centuries on social life and even politics.

My emphasis here is on specialty coffee, but with numerous references to the whole industry, including "conventional" or "commodity" coffee, as in grocery store plastic tubs, and robusta. The coffee trade can be divided into categories, but they go together to form the whole story of the trade, while the price of one type affects the prices of the others.

Once you have had really good coffee, lesser beans seem woefully inadequate if not outright bad. I am spoiled; I don't drink coffee in restaurants unless I'm desperate. Don't speak to me about the greatness of Italian coffee in general; I've had wonderful espresso there but also lousy stuff made with poor quality coffee already ground and stale in a can. Cups like that have about as much interest for me as wet sawdust. Yet robusta or poorer grade arabica, destined for instant coffee or cheaper grocery store blends, certainly has an important place among all coffees.

I refer frequently to Honduras as a case study for both problems and advances in growing and processing coffee. On the one hand, the country is up and coming, despite violence in some regions and stubborn political difficulties. The people I have dealt with there have been uniformly wonderful to me. On the other hand, Honduras has been hit particularly hard by coffee leaf rust; as a result, some of the most intensive work on coffee agriculture, including hybridization, goes on there.

Above all, I want to introduce general readers anywhere to the story of growing, processing, roasting, and brewing my favorite beverage. But I also hope that this book will serve as a concise guide for people in the coffee industry about the product they love, from the ground up, from south to north. I devote particular attention to the most recent research on topics ranging from the effects of coffee on health—almost entirely good, even amazing, news—to what should be in the water used to make coffee, to specialized lab work, and to experiments with hybrids in the field. The reader will kindly keep in mind that research on coffee is broad, deep, and constantly revealing new specific information, if not entirely new vistas. I offer here a frame from one point in a rapidly expanding video.

Passages in italics are intended to provide information about how to make and store coffee, experiments you can do at home, things you should not try there or anywhere else, and assorted other tips about coffee.

Enjoy a great and marvelously important drink, feel good about the product you are consuming, help the earth and farmers, maybe gain a little sophistication—what's not to like about all that? Grab the best cup of coffee you can get and read on.

2

In Producing Countries

Coffee from Farm to Port

They've got an awful lot of coffee in Brazil.

—from "The Coffee Song," Bob Hilliard/Dick Miles
(sung most famously by Frank Sinatra in 1946)

The word *coffee* refers to a tree, to the "beans" (actually the seeds from the plant's fruit), and to beverages made from the beans. In the coffee industry, the term *liquor* means any kind of coffee to drink made by infusion, as in a French press; by forcing water through ground beans, as in espresso; or by allowing gravity to do most of the work, as in drip. *Liquor* means without anything added. Espresso-based drinks like lattes use coffee liquor, of course, and add a lot of milk.

Coffee plants can grow to a height of 15 meters (nearly 50 feet) if not *capped* or *crowned*. In the producing countries, the trees are tended, their fruit is harvested, and at least the initial stages of processing take place. After several layers of material are removed from around the beans, they are called *green* in English (in Spanish *oro*, "gold"). Green coffee has not been roasted. Beans in this form are usually put into jute sacks, sometimes with plastic liners, then into containers, and shipped abroad for roasting. Some especially expensive green coffees are vacuum-packed for shipping. When coffee is roasted in producing countries, then shipped, there is a risk that it will become stale before reaching the consumer. Again, using vacuum-packed bags may avert staling, but that procedure entails serious investments in equipment and in the bags themselves.

Measurements for coffee have evolved into an odd mix. First, beans are sold around the world in dollars per pound. A *bag* of green coffee has a specific meaning and is a standard weight, 60 kilos or 132 pounds, although a bag is 65 kilos from some Latin American countries. Most calculations of how much coffee any country produces, exports, imports, or uses in drinks are expressed in number of bags. International trade may also be measured in tonnes, as in metric ton (1,000 kilos, or about 2,205 pounds). The numbers and trends in coffee sales and consumption can be found at the International Coffee Organization's website, http://www.ico.org.

A measured American cup is eight ounces by volume, not weight. Extraction of liquor by any method is best based on a ratio of ground coffee to water by weight, most easily figured in grams. Central Americans talk about production in terms of *quintals* harvested per *manzana*. A quintal is supposed to be 100 pounds, yet even that varies a little from country to country. And there is no standard manzana. In Argentina (not a coffee country) it is one hectare (abbreviated ha); in Honduras, the word means about 1.73 acres, or almost .7 hectare. All of this makes trying to figure out production and its costs a messy task.

I like to make coffee at a ratio of 15 grams of water per gram of ground coffee, so I use a kitchen scale, which can be handy for other purposes too. To make a more or less regular cup, close to 8 fluid ounces, I use 16 grams of ground coffee and, pouring on water just off the boil, bring the total weight in a mug to 240 grams. In thinking about coffee, there is no need to constantly translate grams or kilos into ounces or pounds; pretty much the only number I have locked in my head is the one for a standard bag of green coffee. A 15:1 ratio by weight makes a pretty strong (a much-abused word in the industry; here it just means the relatively high ratio of coffee to water) cup of coffee, so experiment at home to find your preferred ratio.

A simpler formula is 2 rounded tablespoons per 6–8 ounces (by volume) of water. Extraction time is a function of grain size of the ground coffee, amount of coffee, and type of brewer. Aim for three to four minutes for extraction in most devices.

The idea of fresh roasted coffee can be overrated. In whole-bean form in a sealed bag with a one-way valve, which lets gases from roasted coffee escape but does not allow oxygen in, several months can go by before the beans lose much taste. Once the bag is opened, there are still several weeks to enjoy the flavor—if the beans have merit to begin with. The biggest problem with staling occurs when coffee is ground before being sold. Even the valve won't help much in that case, as ground coffee starts to oxidize and lose flavor immediately. We will return to how to make good coffee in a shop or at home, but meanwhile:

Get a burr grinder, which feeds the beans between two ridged plates, metal or ceramic; nix to a chopper with a blade that cuts the beans. Cutting the beans can reheat the coffee (not good!) and produce varied grain sizes, which makes extraction more chancy. Take a few seconds to grind beans just before making a cup of coffee. Beware of cheap burr grinders, which can jam easily and may not grind well for espresso.

I don't like the idea of keeping coffee in the fridge or freezer, unless you use it really slowly. Opening and closing the fridge or freezer door can produce humidity on the beans, which can lead to flavor loss. It's better just to roll the bag down tightly over the remaining coffee, close the bag with a rubber band or clamp, and put it in a cupboard. However, some recent studies indicate that freezing does not harm beans.

WHERE AND HOW COFFEE GROWS

Almost all specialists on the plant think that the better species, *Coffea arabica*, originated as an understory tree in the highlands of Ethiopia and South Sudan.

Looking down into a burr grinder, the metal grinding plates are visible. Here the top plate has been disassembled to reveal the lower, fixed plate. The screws allow removal and replacement of the burrs, which normally last for years. A chopper, mistakenly called a grinder, typically has a removable cup at the top. Under that is the cutting blade.

Photo by Robert Thurston

Coffee still grows wild in Ethiopia, a fact that is important for our story in general. The coffee plant family is *Rubiaceae*, which is often called the coffee, madder, or bedstraw family. Most of the thousands of species in the family are flowering plants—for instance, gardenias or West Indian jasmine. In order to get fruit set of any kind, a tree has to flower, and coffee certainly does.

With a few exceptions, coffee trees grow in the tropics, between 23½ degrees north and south of the equator. We use the term *arabica*, not *africana*, because Europeans bought their first coffee from Arab merchants in the seventeenth century and thought that it all came from Yemen. Although more than a hundred species of coffee exist, arabica and robusta together amount to well over 90 percent of the world's coffee crop and more than that of all drinks made. Arabica in the twelve months October 2015–October 2016 composed about 64 percent of all coffee shipped, and robusta most of the rest; in recent decades, robusta's share has increased.

Arabica needs some altitude to grow properly, generally 600 to 1,500 meters above sea level, an altitude of roughly 2,000 to 5,000 feet. But great coffee grows in the Kona region of Hawaii as low as 800 feet (244 meters), because clouds roll daily around the south side of the Big Island (also called Hawaii, for the sake of confusion) to shade the trees, and because the island sits right at the Tropic of Cancer. If the Hawaiian Islands were any lower in latitude, that is, closer to the equator, arabica could not grow so close to sea level. In some Central American growing regions, coffee can flourish at 6,000 feet (1,830 meters); in Peru, some trees do all right at 9,500 feet (2,896 meters). The equator touches the northern tip of the country, affording its high fields a little more protection from cold than they would get if they were farther from the center of the tropics.

Arabica trees need lots of water, 60–80 inches (1,500–2,000 millimeters) per year, and then a dry period. If the wet and dry times don't alternate pretty neatly, there will be extra trouble with pests or taste in the cup. Flowering typically takes place after the first rain following a dry spell; irrigation can substitute for rainfall. Frost for even one night can heavily damage or kill arabica trees.

Robusta originated in Central Africa; it shares a common ancestor with arabica. Although tougher in general, robusta is more susceptible to cold than arabica, and it needs more water. Hence it is usually confined to a belt 15 degrees north and south of the equator. Still, robusta can grow where arabica can't, for instance at low altitudes in Liberia or in much of Vietnam. Robusta can

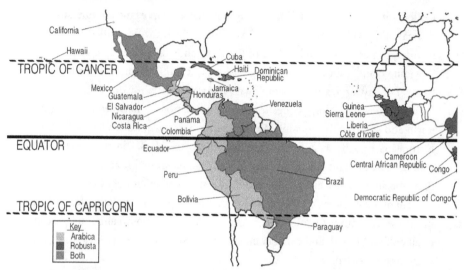

Key
Arabica
Robusta
Both

Where coffee grows around the world.
Map prepared by Lara Thurston

withstand drought and higher temperatures better than its more delicate relative. Less susceptible to pests and diseases, robusta also requires less care and
input in the form of fertilizer and pesticides than arabica. Some small producers
in Mexico, for example, are switching from arabica to robusta because the price
they receive for either species is not much different, and because robusta needs
less maintenance and less fertilizer.

On average, robusta has about twice the caffeine content of arabica but half
the sugar (sucrose in particular). Arabica also has more trigonelline, an alkaloid
that, while bitter by itself, contributes strongly to the formation of pleasant
aroma compounds in the cup. But these substances vary widely within both species and each variety (sub-species) of coffee. In the cup, robusta is often harsh,
rarely subtle; the flavor notes that characterize good arabica are almost always
missing in robusta. Nonetheless, the tough stuff has its passionate adherents,
both as a crop and as a drink.

Arabica trees thrive when daily temperatures rarely rise above the low 80s F
(up to 30°C) and the average temperature is around 62°F. Wind is critical. Too
much at the wrong time will blow flowers off the trees and prevent fruit set. Too
little and the undersides of the leaves may not dry out, leaving a hospitable site
for harmful fungi.

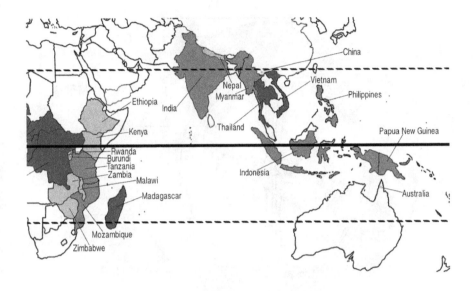

Altitude is in effect a temperature variable. Growing coffee at higher altitudes, depending on how far a farm is from the equator, produces denser beans. *SHB* is a Central American designation meaning "strictly hard bean." Cultivated at altitudes of 5,000 to 6,000 feet or more, such beans develop more slowly and can have a higher sugar content than beans cultivated at lower altitudes. High-grown coffee can have more intense flavors, but since many factors go into the "quality" of a cup, SHB or similar terms do not automatically mean the coffee is better. Many superb beans come from lower elevations.

Coffee can be cultivated in a wide range of soil types, most often volcanic in origin. The trees do well in loam, which has about the same proportion of sand and clay in the soil, with silt to a lesser degree. The grain size of silt is between that of rough sand and fine clay. Together, these materials provide drainage (sand), hold moisture (clay), and hold nutrients (silt). So if the temperature range is right, the wind does its job properly, the soil is in good shape and holds nutrients well, pesticides and nutrients are supplied regularly and on time in the yearly cycle, the altitude is appropriate, and the farmer is skilled, arabica has a chance to grow.

Inside the coffee fruit two separate beans—actually embryos—usually develop. These are half-round on one side and flat on the other. When one seed

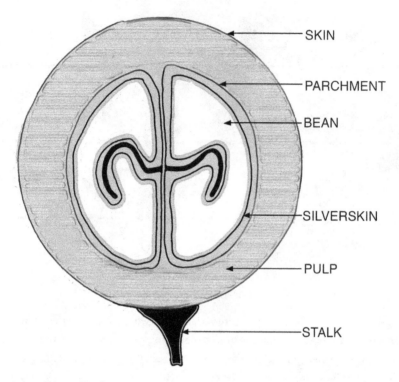

Parts of the coffee fruit.
Illustration by Lara Thurston

does not develop, largely because of poor pollination, the other will expand and become round. The bean is then known as peaberry. These berries may be 10 percent of any crop, occasionally rising to 30 percent. Some consumers prize them, although their taste profiles vary and do not stand out as necessarily superior. Because of their shape and relative uniformity, peaberries are somewhat easier to roast evenly than their flat-sided brethren.

The genetic base of today's arabica is terribly narrow. I have asked scientists to give me a figure for genetic variability—2 percent? 5 percent? It appears that no one knows and that perhaps the question is not important. Suffice it to say that the genetic distance among arabica plants discovered so far is small, which opens the way for disastrous epidemics. A lethal fungus, *Hemileia vastatrix*, coffee leaf rust (in Spanish *la roya*), spread around the world in the 1860s and 1870s, killing nearly all arabica trees. Since then coffee plants have descended from pockets of trees that somehow survived, perhaps because of particular lo-cal conditions. Arabica on the island in the Indian Ocean once called Bourbon, now Réunion, is considered the progenitor of the variety called 'Bourbon.' Some other trees, in parts of Java and elsewhere, also survived the pandemic. From such hardier or luckier plants, we get the variety called 'Typica.' Between these two closely related types, coffee once more circled the globe.

Neither variety returned to all the areas where it had grown previously, nota-bly skipping Sri Lanka (then Ceylon), which switched to tea cultivation. Almost all the other useful varieties around now—'Caturra', 'Catuai', 'Pacas', and many others—have arisen as mutations of 'Bourbon' or 'Typica', through selective breeding of those two, or through crosses with robusta. The overrated Jamaican Blue Mountain, for instance, is a 'Typica' offshoot. Occasionally a new variety will appear, or perhaps be rediscovered; this is the story of the coveted 'Gesha' or 'Geisha', found growing untended on a Panamanian farm in the early 2000s. Also originally from Ethiopia, this variety shares coffee's narrow genetic base.

Since coffee is largely self-pollinating, and because arabica and robusta are closely related species, they can crossbreed. In 1917 this happened spontane-ously, on the Indonesian island of Timor (not to be confused with the inde-pendent country of East Timor). The resulting plant is called 'Hybrido de Timor'. From it many other hybrids have been developed; the ending -mor, like 'Catimor' or 'Sarchimor', indicates a variety descended from that trans-species cross. These coffees are hardier than ones derived solely from arabica lines, but in general the '-mors' have not matched the cup quality of other coffees that are "more arabica."

The worst enemy of coffee today, at least in Latin America, is that same leaf rust. Arabica hybridization is in a race against rust, which mutates quickly, as often as every two weeks. New hybrids that at first were not susceptible to the fungus can lose their resistance over time; this happened in 2017 to the 'Lem-pira' variety in Honduras. Different "races" of roya appear quickly and spread from country to country.

Rust fungus starts with spots on leaves and can cause entire branches to drop their leaves, eventually killing the tree. The disease reappeared in Brazil in 1970 but did not then become a huge problem. A far deadlier assault began in Colombia in 2008. From there, rust spread north across Central America into Mexico by 2012, only to turn back south to Peru and Ecuador in 2013. Rust's

Rust on a leaf of a coffee plant.
Photo courtesy of World Coffee Research, Flor Amarilla, Honduras

effects were aggravated by poor farming practices, among them diminished application of fertilizer, a reaction to low prices for the crop and farmers' declining income. Another factor was "higher minimum/lower maximum temperatures (+0.1°C/–0.5°C on average during 2008–2011 [than occurred earlier] . . . in Chinchiná, Colombia)," for example. The same pattern appeared in Guatemala in 2012.[1] Such changes allowed roya more time in a latent stage. From there it burst forth with special intensity.

The Colombian coffee crop suffered terribly, falling as much as 31 percent in the epidemic years. In other Latin American regions, the loss was from 15 to 40 percent. From 2012 to 2016, rust caused estimated losses of over $2.5 billion in green coffee production and 1.75 million jobs in Guatemala, El Salvador, Honduras, Costa Rica, Panama, the Dominican Republic, and Jamaica.[2] Guatemala, Honduras, and El Salvador declared coffee rust a national emergency in 2013. The most drastic remedy for rust was to rip out affected trees and replace them with hardier hybrids. Replanting was beyond the means of many small farmers, who, if they continued to grow arabica at all, relied on government aid and agronomists' help to start over with new trees.

In the recent epidemic, trees that were well fertilized and also under some shade survived more often than their poorly tended cousins or coffee under full sun. However, as we will see, the issue of shade is now in question. High plant density, 10,000 or more per hectare, created excellent conditions for the spread of rust, as close proximity results in higher temperature and humidity around the trees. It is also more difficult to spray adequately among closely packed plants. To deal effectively with rust, or for that matter with most pests, using either bio- or synthetic mixtures, the undersides of the leaves must be sprayed.

In an effort to avoid a repetition of the rust crisis, and to have the chance to replant trees should a pandemic again hit coffee, biologists have been compiling seed banks and repositories. Teams are searching the highlands of Ethiopia for forest trees with previously unknown genetic material. Arabica seeds are "recalcitrant," meaning that they lose their vitality if their moisture content becomes too low. Thus arabica samples cannot be kept in vitro or in cold storage; they have to be planted in fields. Thirty such sites that preserve coffee germ plasm exist, in Ethiopia, Costa Rica, Kenya, El Salvador, and elsewhere. However, several such fields are underfunded and in danger of collapsing.

Hybridization of arabica plants is now the subject of major funding and research. Important new findings for work with hybrids appeared with the sequencing of the genomes of both robusta and arabica, as mentioned earlier. Suspicion immediately surfaced when the UC Davis findings were announced; a researcher from Davis told me he received a complaint that "I don't want any genes in my coffee." Probably the person meant "No GMO [genetically modified organism] coffee."

GMO is sometimes called transgenic or genetic engineering. In some food crops, scientists have inserted a gene from an organism of one species into the DNA of another. Ever since settled agriculture began, traditional breeding techniques for plants or animals have altered their offspring's DNA. That has been a hit-and-miss process; genetic engineering in labs is precise. But scientists at Davis and elsewhere have told me they are not working on GMO coffee, and none is for sale anywhere now.

Instead, identifying the genetic sequence of coffee species helps in focusing on genetic markers. Researchers expect that markers will greatly shorten the time for the creation of useful new hybrids. If a genetic marker is known to indicate that a certain plant is resistant to rust, for example, then that plant may be used as a parent in hybridization. Other plants without the marker are not used, and much time and guesswork is eliminated. Researchers also hope that markers can help in developing plants with good cup quality.

World Coffee Research (WCR), a new organization with ties to researchers around the world, is conducting experiments in hybridization using arabica and -mor varieties. At Flor Amarilla, WCR's farm in El Salvador, arabica plants are crossed both with robusta and with Ethiopian forest trees selected for their hardiness and relative genetic distance from the other parent. A successful new hybrid with heterosis, or hybrid vigor, obtained in this way is called an F1 (for first generation) plant. Forty-six useful crosses have resulted so far; they are growing at Flor Amarilla and in Rwanda. More test plots are planned around the world.

Workers in El Salvador and elsewhere, for example at La Fe in Honduras, use an office hole punch to take dots of leaf material from these hybrids. Labs then clone entire plants from the dots. Simply planting F1 seeds doesn't work well, as it produces a bewildering range of offspring, of which only a few will match the F1 parents; other descendants will have entirely different, often useless, characteristics.

The cross breeding then continues: cloned F1s are paired again with Ethiopian forest trees. Researchers seek to create plants that are rust resistant, productive, and have good cup quality. Since the trees at WCR were planted in 2016, it may take a decade or more before the investigators have the results they seek in a single variety. And genotype is not phenotype; the second term means the way an organism expresses its genetic qualities as it grows and matures. We need to know how hybrids behave on commercial farms.

WCR has also identified 1,216 fungi that live on or around coffee trees and is working on using some of them to fight rust, as they eat rust spores on leaves. Nematodes, tiny roundworms, attack roots and rob plants of vitality. WCR is busy grafting arabica trunks onto robusta roots, which are much stronger and can resist nematodes. In another important advance, the organization will certify the "health and purity" of its coffee seeds. Growers can be confident that a certified variety is in fact resistant to rust, for example, at the time it leaves a nursery.[3]

An F1 hybrid with high survivability and high productivity recently received 90.5 points in Nicaragua's Cup of Excellence competition, a country-based way of promoting quality that has spread across Latin America. The score indicates excellent if not quite exceptional coffee. The winning variety, 'Centroamericano', is much more resistant to nematodes, rust, and coffee berry disease than its parents or other local varieties are.[4]

Another severe problem in numerous coffee lands is food security: having something to eat all year round. Spanish has the expression *los meses flacos*, "the thin months," to describe hunger and even starvation among coffee families and workers when money from the last harvest runs out. Recent surveys have found that in Mexico and Guatemala, more than 50 percent of coffee-growing families experience food insecurity each year; in Nicaragua, the figure is about 87 percent. This situation exists even on farms that produce Fair Trade and/or organic coffee.[5] (More discussion of these certification and buying programs follows.) Much work by governments and NGOs addresses hunger, for example, by introducing new food intercrops to grow among coffee trees, building better food storage facilities to prevent loss to rodents and insects, and creating vegetable and compost bins.

Hondurans recently assured me that food security is not a problem for the country's coffee farmers. This view may be overoptimistic for the country as a whole; a 2014 report by CARE estimated that 60 percent of Hondurans suffer from hunger and malnutrition. Yet, mirroring the positive attitude I encountered so often there, farmers "are enhancing their productivity, diversifying their crops and accessing domestic and international markets to break the cycle of poverty. As their incomes rise, they are able to purchase [and grow, I would add] more nutritious food for their families." Honduras cut its hunger rate in half from 2000 to 2015.[6]

How coffee is grown makes a considerable difference in how much farmers earn, in how much pesticide and insecticide they must use, and in crop diversification. Shade is a good place to begin; it can help in various ways but hardly solves all the crop's problems. In recent years, shade-grown coffee has gained in reputation. For coffee that likes shade in the first place, 50–60 percent luminosity has been considered ideal. But WCR has recently found that shade may encourage the spread of rust, which needs some moisture to survive, because leaves dry out less well in shade.[7]

Many types of trees can provide shade on coffee farms. There may be big old native denizens that producers never removed, despite the advice of agronomists in the 1970s, or anything deliberately planted, from the Mexican *shimbillo* tree to plantains and bananas. Shade trees must be pruned to allow the right amount of sunlight through for a given coffee variety, meaning that extra labor is involved.

Shade provides other important benefits, hence the appeal of shade-grown or "bird-friendly" coffee. Next to natural forest, coffee farms with significant shade are the best habitat for birds migrating north-south in the Americas. Large trees shelter coffee from strong winds and rain, especially at altitudes above 1,800 meters (nearly 6,000 feet); help prevent soil erosion; hamper weed growth on the ground; provide organic matter as they drop leaves and branches; keep more moisture in the soil; and host helpful creatures, from spiders to small animals. Bees like some shade, and although arabica is largely self-pollinating or draws pollen from wind, bees can be important. A new report from the U.S. Academy of Sciences argues that not only is bee pollination significant for coffee right now, it will become more important as the earth warms. In the Academy's science-speak, "Although we found reduced coffee suitability and bee species diversity for more than one-third of the future coffee-suitable areas, all future coffee-suitable areas will potentially host at least five bee species, indicating continued pollination services. Bee diversity also can be expected to offset farmers' losses from reduced coffee suitability."[8] Farmers should therefore look to ways that bee habitat can be enhanced.

Can birds help coffee? A "bird exclusion" study in the Blue Mountain region of Jamaica used nets to keep birds away from stands of coffee trees, while other, unprotected fields served as the control group. Researchers found that birds can reduce the number of coffee berry borers (Spanish *broca*) by as much as 14 percent. These hungry insects feed inside coffee fruit as they develop, ruining it in the process, and opening tunnels to the seeds that allow fungus to enter.[9] Alas, even the fields with birds still suffered much from the borer. It has spread in recent decades to all producing lands, has climbed higher in altitude, and reproduces faster than before; losses from the pest are estimated at $500 million a year.

Several other common agricultural practices help protect and nurture coffee trees. Mulching between them preserves moisture and keeps weeds from robbing the coffee of nutrients and water. The best mulch also contributes some fertilizer. Weeds are not always coffee's mortal enemy; some weedy plants also conserve moisture and reduce soil erosion. Certain cover crops serve the same functions—for example, Greenleaf desmodium, a tropical legume that I know as beggars' lice. Desmodium requires careful seeding and maintenance, but it can also be useful as cattle fodder.

The worst weeds do contend with the coffee plants for nutrients and water, especially in dry periods. Nothing stops all intruders. Therefore, farmers have to either attack weeds with hand tools, entailing a lot of labor, or they must spray. Both bio-sprays and synthetic ones can be expensive.

Like all fruit trees, coffee must be pruned carefully to remain productive. First, the trees should be capped at 1.6–1.8 meters (5.25–6 feet). That height allows workers to reach all ripe cherries and facilitates spraying and pruning around the whole tree. After two yield cycles, dead or unproductive branches (usually lower ones) need to be cut back. The basically delicate arabica tree can and should be treated roughly at this point. Drastic pruning is essential. If left entirely to themselves, as many still are in the Ethiopian highlands, arabica trees do not produce well. No coffee tree is efficient at bearing fruit if left in its natural state. Mature trees are most productive for five or six years at the longest; they will then be "stumped." That involves cutting the trunk at either 25–30 centimeters or 50 centimeters above the ground. Suckers later emerge from the stump. Farmers then select the strongest sucker and remove the others. New branches may be trained to grow up, not allowed to sprawl down toward the ground. In another two years, branches from the new trunk will bear usable fruit. This cycle can be repeated until the tree ages past its prime, at twenty-five to thirty years old.

ORGANIC VS. SYNTHETIC: YES, COFFEE IS FULL OF CHEMICALS

The U.S. Department of Agriculture (USDA) says that, "Organic food is produced without using most conventional pesticides; fertilizers made with synthetic ingredients or sewage sludge; bioengineering; or ionizing radiation." Soil amendments not found in nature, along with many synthetic sprays, may not be used. Naturally occurring materials—for instance, guano (seabird excrement)—are allowed. Agriculture everywhere was "organic" until synthetic fertilizers and pesticides became widely available after World War II.

The USDA forbids *most* conventional pesticides but approves others in some situations. For example, chlorine and lignin sulfonate, a dust-control agent synthetically derived from lignin, a naturally occurring polymer in wood, are permitted. Rotenone, an organic substance obtained from the roots of tropical plants, may be spread on organic fields as an insecticide, although it kills fish if it reaches their habitat. Organic farmers are unfettered in other ways as well; for example, they may use flame-throwing devices on weeds.

"Organic" is not a way of doing without chemicals. Everything is composed of chemicals, including every food you eat, everything you touch, and you the reader. There is no "chemical-free makeup," although a search for it returns many hits. Likewise "organic chemical-free decaf coffee" is nonsense. Various labels insist that their decaffeinated coffee is "organic," not just because of how it was grown but also because it was decaffeinated without "chemicals"—that is, simply by using water to carry away the caffeine. Yet water is a chemical; the air anywhere, no matter how clean, consists of chemicals.

The chemical structure of any organic compound can be the same as that of any nonorganic one. Elements, the most basic chemicals of all, which are listed in the periodic table, are always the same. Nitrogen is nitrogen, whether it is found in bird excrement or is fixed, in the form of ammonia, from the air in an industrial process. Likewise, nitrogen combined with other elements can be "organic" or not.

All plants, grown organically or "conventionally," need fertilizer. Fertilizer may be as simple as the age-old standby, manure, or as complicated as the big chemical companies can make it. Above all, a combination of nitrogen, phosphorus, and potassium (NPK) is needed for healthy plants. Nitrogen helps the vegetative growth of the trees, namely the trunk and leaves. Phosphorus is important for roots, wood in general, and young buds of shoots and branches. Potassium helps with the development of fruit.

Guano contains a lot of organic NPK. But there isn't much of it left lying around. It used to be mined on seacoasts and islands, especially off the coast of Peru, where it had been accumulating for centuries. By the 1870s, most of the readily accessible guano had been stripped from the islands, although some mining goes on to this day.

The Haber-Bosch process, developed in Germany in 1913, made it possible to synthesize ammonia from air, and from there to obtain nitrogen and nitrates. Now fertilizers could be manufactured, although that did not happen on a large scale until the late 1940s.

Back in the fields, NPK and trace elements taken up by plants have to be replaced in the soil if agriculture is to be sustainable. In centuries past, whole villages might move to a new area, clear it of trees, burn the stumps, and begin to grow crops again. This "slash-and-burn" agriculture still takes place in some parts of the Amazonian rain forest, for example, where it quickly devastates the earth. Elsewhere, farmers need to make their soil last.

The ironically named "green revolution" took hold in many parts of the world in the 1960s and '70s, including in coffee lands. Scientists urged farmers to cut down all trees and bushes in the fields, plant new hybrid varieties of crops that tolerated full sun, and feed and protect them with synthetic products. At first, productivity for many crops per land unit went way up in some cases, as much as 300 percent for varieties of corn (maize) and rice.[10] For coffee, the increase was not nearly so great. And the cost of synthetic pesticides and fertilizers added a lot to farm expenses.

The new plants were supposed to be better able to withstand leaf rust, and for a while they did. But rust mutates rapidly. After a number of years, resistance can be overcome or bypassed and the plants wither or die again, as the case of 'Lempira' showed. When that cycle occurred in the 1970s and '80s, it caused serious distrust between the farmers who planted the hybrids and the agronomists who touted them.

Many coffee farmers have little choice about whether to go organic. Small producers in Chiapas, Mexico, for example, can't afford to buy industrial sprays and fertilizers, so they have to be organic. They grow coffee under partial shade because they can gather other products, such as nuts or wood, from the big trees.

Farther south, in Costa Rica, it can rain for days at a time—the wrong time—making it next to impossible for the undersides of coffee leaves to dry out. Again, that makes a hospitable environment for coffee leaf rust, leaving farmers with two options: to spray heavily with synthetic products, or to let their trees die.

Organic production entails other difficulties in many cases. Studies comparing conventional and organic farms in Central America have found that on average organic is less productive, as measured by coffee harvested per hectare, labor inputs, and net income of the farmers (gross income minus all costs). Organic farms produced 28 percent less in one investigation in Mexico and 44 percent in another; 33 percent less in Nicaragua; and 43 percent in one Costa Rican case and 22 percent in still another. Yields were roughly equal in Guatemala and just 2 percent lower for Honduras. The last two results may indicate problems on conventional farms more than successes in organic farming.[11]

One study comparing pairs of small Costa Rican farms, chosen because they were of similar size and located near each other, found that *some* organic operations did produce as well as conventional cultivation. But when the cost of certification was figured into net income, the organic farmers earned less money than the conventional farmers did. The researchers calculated that to make net income the same for both types of farms, "the price premiums paid to organic producers would have to increase to 38%," well above the average in the study of 20 percent. Some organic farmers received no premiums at all.[12]

For many growers, organic certification is difficult to obtain; they must fill out many forms over a period of at least three years, their soil must be tested, and they must keep careful records. Becoming certified may involve extensive paperwork and interaction with several government agencies. Corruption and creation of false documents for organic are far from unknown.[13] Organic requires more labor than conventional farming; while conventional involves considerable labor in spraying and applying fertilizer, there is a trade-off in weed control. On certified organic farms, it must be done by hand or with flaming devices, and that makes for a lot of work.[14] Everyone must prune trees carefully.

A severe critique of organic coffee farming comes from Dr. H. A. M. van der Vossen, a "plant breeding and seed specialist" from the Netherlands. In 2005 he argued that "to sustain economically viable yield levels [at least one tonne, 1,000 kilograms, of green coffee per hectare per year] large additional amounts of composted organic matter will have to come from external sources" and that "most smallholders will be unable to acquire such quantities and have to face declining yields." Organic farming is not necessarily effective in reducing the impact of diseases and pests to an economically tolerable level, while trees under heavy shade are more humid than those in sun and thus may raise the incidence of rust or other problems.[15]

Van der Vossen's conclusions may be too harsh. The benefits of shade trees on coffee farms, however limited, have been discussed above. Organic farms can have other cash or food crops, among them bananas or plantains, flowers, and hardwoods, growing beside or among coffee trees.

Certainly organic coffee agriculture does succeed in numerous parts of the world. The International Federation of Organic Agriculture Movements (IFOAM) asserts that, "The data available clearly points to significant yield increases when smallholders in East Africa adopt organic agriculture practices." Profits for exports also rise, the report continues, with organic practices in the region. However, no specific data on productivity or income are given for coffee. The document cites, without criticism, findings by van der Vossen and other writers who have identified lower productivity and income from coffee in Latin America. Instead, IFOAM argues that conditions in Africa are significantly different, such that moving from conventional farming to organic involves little additional cost.[16] This view is reminiscent of the situation of coffee farmers in Mexico, who are often too poor to buy synthetic sprays or soil amendments. Thus the judgment of organic coffee's economic viability from IFOAM sounds familiar: organic works when its cost, in money or productivity, is not too high.

Yet I have seen organic coffee farms that work extremely well. An example is the farm Selva Negra, located near Matagalpa, Nicaragua. This farm/resort/ meeting/wedding center has become all but completely self-sufficient in energy use and waste management in recent years; for example, pigs are raised organically, and their manure produces methane gas, which is collected and used to cook pork dishes in the estate's restaurant. Hot water comes from solar collectors, and wastewater is treated and used for irrigation. In addition, the owner-manager, Mausi Kuhl, makes sure that her workers are well treated. The same pickers return each year and stay in decent housing while on the farm. After spending several days there recently, I can testify that Selva Negra is a pretty happy and beautiful place. However, the availability of income streams besides coffee sales helps the farm flourish.

Is organic food better nutritionally, or does it taste better than conventionally grown or GMO products? Even organic.org has to admit on the first question that "no definitive research . . . makes this claim." Regarding taste, the same website says only that "taste is definitely an individual matter."[17] Some organic coffees have received 97 of a possible 100 points from the highly respected e-journal *Coffee Review*, but so have some conventional coffees. Organic coffee agriculture therefore has to do above all with conditions for the earth and farmers, not with the quality of the coffee or health risks in drinking it. Chapter 4 will return to the issue of coffee and health.

Whatever is put on the fields in coffee farming does not change the natural wrappings around the seeds: skin, mucilage, parchment, and silverskin. Those protective layers mean that insecticides and pesticides of any kind do not usually penetrate the beans. In any event, a review of the research in 2012 concluded that when low levels of residue were found in some samples of green coffee, they "were reduced to insignificant amounts during the roasting process."[18] Heating beans to 380°F (closing in on 200°C) or higher gets rid of any impurities, however rare they may have been in the first place.

Much of the verbiage around "organic" is unhelpful. Everyone wants clean air, water, and soil. People seek good health for everyone from pickers to chief executives. Consumers, agronomists, and farmers want beans and beverages that are good for people. But to pit organic against conventional is not the best way to discuss farming.

"Sustainable" and "best practices" are two better ideas in thinking about agriculture. *Sustainable* can be defined in a quick and direct way or in oceans of ink. At its simplest, the word means treating the environment with techniques and substances that allow agriculture to continue in one place indefinitely. Don't

Mausi Kuhl, matriarch of Selva Negra, Nicaragua, in a relaxed moment.
Photo by Robert Thurston

take more out of the earth than goes back into it. Don't degrade the soil and pollute the water to the extent that cultivation declines or can no longer take place.

The U.S. Congress offered a longer definition in the Farm Bill of 1990:

> Sustainable agriculture means an integrated system of plant and animal production practices having a site-specific application that will, over the long term satisfy human food and fiber needs; enhance environmental quality and the natural resource base upon which the agricultural economy depends; make the most efficient use of nonrenewable resources and on-farm resources and integrate, where appropriate, natural biological cycles and controls; sustain the economic viability of farm operations; and enhance the quality of life for farmers and society as a whole.[19]

Note that the word "organic" is absent. The phrase "natural biological cycles and controls" is mysterious, as nothing in agriculture has remained the way nature set it out originally. Other parts of the "definition" reflect the desire of Congress to extend best wishes to the world.

"Good agricultural practices" relate to both sustainability and safety. For example, farms should have a plan and facilities in place to deal with runoff, both from pesticides and animal waste. There should be an "integrated pest management plan," as the Ontario Ministry of Agriculture, Food, and Rural Affairs puts it,[20] among numerous other points. None of this excludes some use of synthetic sprays and soil amendments.

Organic practices do not help farmers withstand a severe outbreak of broca or roya. In fact, as the respected coffee buyer and writer Thompson Owen of the company Sweet Maria's has seen in Central America, "The real impact [of rust] is on organic farms, whether certified farms or organic-by-default farms, on casual coffee farmers who have little technical knowledge, and on smallholder farms in general."[21] The co-op Asociación Chajulense in Guatemala, where 90 percent of the farmers grow organic and the rest are working toward certification, has also reported great difficulties in fighting rust.[22] Ric Rhinehart, executive director of the Specialty Coffee Association, has made similar comments about the connection between organic and rust.[23]

Besides roya and broca, a host of other pests attack the plants. Most are limited to certain areas of the world, especially Africa. They may spread at some point. There are, for example, the antestia bug, fried egg scales (now well controlled by local ladybird beetles), the coffee twig borer in Asia, and even more exotic creatures like the coffee berry butterfly, sometimes called the playboy. Nematodes have already been mentioned. If an infestation of broca is not too bad, farmers can control the insect by bio methods, as shown in the next photo. Workers cut windows in the sides of 2-liter soft drink bottles, put some sweet poison in the bottom, and hang the traps among the coffee trees. A lot of broca find their way into the traps. Controlling fried egg scales with beetles is a wonderful, bio way of defeating a pest. Still, sprays of some kind are the best or only means of dealing with many of coffee's enemies.

How can anyone make money growing coffee? A recent report from the Specialty Coffee Association argues that the answer is rarely simply to increase production. Increasing yield typically "increases the cost per hectare . . . and hence may decrease a farm's profitability." Lowering the costs of growing coffee is probably a better strategy. Production costs should be calculated per hectare, not per pound of green coffee. "Farms investing less than $2000/ha can count on

A bag containing more than 400,000 dead broca insects. They were collected in 400 traps set on 25 manzanas, about 43 acres or 17.5 hectares of land, for fifteen days in central Honduras. The plastic bottle next to the bag is the kind of simple trap hung in or near trees to collect these pests.
Photo by Robert Thurston at La Fe Research Station

making a profit at a variety of yield levels, whereas coffee farms that invest more than $2000/ha require high yields and/or high prices to achieve profitability. On average, production cost per pound should be $2.50 or less."[24] However, that figure must be set into the local context of market prices for the variety raised.

Any for-profit business should aim to raise revenue and cut or at least control costs. Thus the report sounds logical in considering how to organize a farm and what kind of inputs, at what cost, should go into growing coffee. But so many other factors are involved, as we have seen, in trying to produce a successful crop that the SCA study should be taken as a broad way of thinking about coffee farming. As ads for many products warn, individual results may vary.

COFFEE CULTIVATION

To begin growing coffee, farmers plant seeds in a nursery. After several weeks, each seed puts down a root, then pushes the bean above the soil a few inches. This is the "soldier" or "matchstick" phase, since the little plants can look like rows of helmeted soldiers or like old-style matchsticks, depending on one's imagination. Several small, green leaves then appear from the top of the bean. Most varieties must be protected in the nursery from the direct sun under natural shade or some sort of canopy, a reminder of arabica's origin as an understory tree.

After spending perhaps six to eight months in the nursery, the young coffee plants can graduate to fields. It takes several more years, typically up to four years altogether from the time seeds are planted, before the trees will bear usable fruit. This long maturation period means that farmers must gamble on what the situation will be years after planting seeds or acquiring seedlings. Will the market be viable for the kind of coffee they cultivate? Will there be a considerable oversupply of coffee at that point, as has happened regularly since the 1930s? All agriculture is a gamble on the weather and the market, but coffee represents an extreme case.

Coffee trees should be planted far enough apart to let people pass between them or, on a mechanized farm, for a large truck to pass between rows of plants. Once mature, the trees have to be pruned after each harvest. Cutting away dead branches is simple enough, but to shape a tree for maximum production is more difficult. Coffee flowers, and hence fruit set, the appearance of berries, occur only on new growth along existing branches. Selecting less promising branches

A coffee nursery at the J. Hill Company, Santa Ana, El Salvador.
Photo by Robert Thurston

to cut back is a matter of experience. Again, on mechanized farms, the practice is different: a loud and lethal machine equipped with whirling blades crawls through the fields and cuts the sides and tops of the trees cleanly. That's wasteful but quick, as is true with most ag mechanization, but also more productive in a basic way than using humans with their puny hands and tools.

As noted, coffee trees should be mulched to prevent soil erosion and reduce weed growth and water loss. The ground must also be cleared of all old cherries that have fallen from the trees, because downed fruit is broca's favorite habitat. Any farm needs applications of fertilizer from time to time; there is no possibility of allowing a field of coffee trees to lie fallow or to plow some crop under the trees that returns nutrients to the soil—for example, nitrogen-bearing alfalfa or clover.

Ripping out diseased trees, buying new seedlings, then waiting for years for the trees to bear usable fruit, is not for those with shallow pockets, unless they are getting help from some outside organization. A good example of such aid comes from the Colombian Coffee Growers Federation (Federación Nacional de Cafeteros de Colombia, FNC), one of the oldest national coffee organizations, founded in 1927. The federation operates on a democratic structure, with elected representatives at the local and regional level. Funding comes from contributions, the Juan Valdez brand of coffee and cafés in several countries, enterprises such as hotels, and above all from a duty levied and collected by the organization for each pound of coffee exported. Starting in 2008, the FNC assisted farmers in replacing about three billion trees with varieties better able to withstand pests and rising temperatures. More trees will follow, along with agronomists to advise how to care for them and how to make coffee agriculture more sustainable. Colombia aims to make all coffee farming sustainable by 2027.

The FNC also helps farmers' families with expenses for health insurance, infrastructure improvements, eyeglasses, and more. Since Colombian coffee yields have risen from a low point in 2008, and peace appears likely after years of fighting between government forces and leftist guerrillas, the federation will be able to do even more in the future. Meanwhile, the Colombian Ministry of Tourism is contributing $2 million to the FNC, with the realization that coffee farms and ecotourism go together well. After sitting in a hot tub in Quindio, Colombia, and watching the sun set over the Andes, I couldn't agree more.

By far the largest coffee-producing country is Brazil. In the 2016/17 harvest year, Brazil's output was 56.1 million bags (60 kilos each, we remember, or 132 pounds) of robusta and arabica, down about 4 million bags from the previous year. Next largest in 2016/17 was Vietnam, almost entirely robusta, at 26.7 million, also down from the year before. Colombia produced 14.5 million bags of arabica and none of robusta. Indonesia followed at 10.6 million, of which almost nine-tenths were robusta. Ethiopia rounded out the top five producers at 6.52 million bags of arabica. Some of the best-known growing countries, for instance Kenya, produce relatively little coffee; for 2016/17, the crop was 700,000 bags.[25] Hawaii's output of green coffee is around .04 percent of global output, at less than 150,000 bags annually

Brazil and Vietnam grow immense quantities of robusta. Usually just over a quarter of Brazil's coffee is robusta, called *conilon* there. Some 95–97 percent of Vietnamese coffee is robusta, a figure related to the relatively low altitude of the country. The terrain also puts Vietnam at particular risk for losses in the crop as the earth gets warmer. In 2017, Brazil's conilon production suffered severely due to drought.

All coffee trees must flower in order to have fruit set. Most regions have one flowering and hence one harvest a year; in a few places, for instance, Colombia and Kenya, close to the equator, there may be two periods of flowering and two harvests, one much smaller than the other. Flowering lasts a few weeks. As the flowers dry up, beans appear as tiny oval shapes where the blooms were. Several months later, *some* of the coffee fruit is ready to harvest. If there is only one harvest per year, there will be a cycle of large output one year followed by small output the next. Ripe fruit is called coffee cherry, because when ready to pick it is about the size and color of a cherry, although in some varieties the mature fruit turns yellow.

Coffee trees once grew routinely to a height of 30 or more feet. Before emancipation in 1888, slaves in Brazil used to march out from their miserable housing to the plants balancing long ladders on their shoulders. When the slaves brought coffee back to the main part of a farm, they used heavy wooden mortars and pestles to separate the seeds from the skin and pulp. Sometimes slaves had to climb into large barrels and use their bare feet for the task, much as sentimental old movies showed grape harvesters at work.

A photo of a Brazilian slave working in coffee; in the foreground are baskets and a wooden mortar and pestle used to separate beans from pulp on Brazilian farms into the twentieth century, on display at the Museo do Café (Museum of Coffee), Santos, Brazil.
Photo by Robert Thurston

Now coffee trees are kept to a height that puts them within reach of human or mechanical pickers. Where the terrain is steep and shade is abundant, trees may grow in a kind of jumble, within which the pickers move along the hillsides. Workers sometimes tie themselves to larger trees so that they won't slip down the slope and spill the cherries they have already picked. On that kind of farm, machines are not of much use. Who could run a tractor through a mass of foliage up and down a steep hill?

Some operations cultivate several million trees; each one may be irrigated by a drip hose around the trunk. On a farm of that scale, the coffee will almost invariably be technified. Planting trees in neat rows allows heavy machinery to maneuver among them.

One of the most remarkable and capital-intensive new developments in grow-ing coffee is geospatial farming (GSF). There is some alphabet soup here, but I hope not too much. To use GSF, farm employees start by taking hundreds if not thousands of soil samples from around the fields, for coffee a minimum of one per hectare. The samples are then plotted on a digital topographic map created from aerial photographs supplemented by ground surveys. Leaf samples are also taken; these physical materials might actually be stored somewhere. The sample locations can also be mapped over a Google Earth image of the land. The soil is directly analyzed using an electromagnetic scanner, a small box jammed with sensors that is dragged across the fields by an all-terrain vehicle (ATV). Soil temperatures can also be recorded. Drones can look down on the fields to identify dead trees.

Now the farm managers mate global information systems (GIS) with global positioning systems (GPS). GPS technology allows workers to know exactly where they are on a farm, while GIS draws from the database of soil already created to indicate which parts of the fields are dry, wet, or in need of fertilizer. Even individual trees can be checked in this way.

With all this information stored centrally on the farm, it can be relayed to tractors equipped with computers and dispensers for fertilizer and pesticides. The tractors—still actually driven by human beings—move among the plants and "know," via the computers, when to release fertilizer and at what rate. Areas of a farm are identified in which trees are especially productive or unproduc-tive, which helps the managers decide what to do: add more nutrients, remove problematic trees, or replant.

Two- or three-year-old coffee trees on a steep hillside, La Fe, Honduras.
Photo by Robert Thurston

Even considering the substantial investment required to put all this together and keep it going year after year, overall production costs can fall as much as 30 percent. The savings in fertilizer and water for irrigation are substantial, while overall productivity per tree rises significantly.[26] Certainly many fewer workers, but generally literate and highly trained ones, are employed in this kind of operation.

GIS, if not GSF, is already used on coffee farms in Brazil and elsewhere. Small plots, or those with considerable shade, cannot logically or economically go full geospatial. The mapping systems have to be able to look at coffee from the air without cloud cover and with only minor distractions from other vegetation; each kind of plant has a specific light signature that is visible and measurable from above, using the right devices.

We would also expect that farms employing geospatial are highly mechanized for harvesting and processing. If little guys survive in the face of increased GSF productivity and lowered costs, it will be because they produce higher quality coffee, and perhaps because more and more consumers will be persuaded to pay above-market prices for their beans.

The other end of coffee gathering—not even agriculture—involves trees growing wild in Ethiopian forests. People can pick ripe cherries from these trees, a laborious and erratic process. In this scenario, little or no input is matched by very low output. Meanwhile, Ethiopia loses forest annually, on average almost 141,000 hectares from 1990 to 2000. Low prices in the coffee crisis years prompted many farmers to switch to *qat*, whose leaves when chewed produce a mild narcotic. Regular users can often be identified by the green drool trickling from their mouths. Thus coffee, itself containing the mild narcotic caffeine, has to compete with other narcotics in Africa and in Latin America, where coca used for cocaine grows.

Who raises coffee? A typical estimate is that 70–80 percent of it comes from small farmers; 25 million is a round guess of their number around the world. To say the least, these people generally do not have a large profit margin or access to loans at low interest rates. The outlines of a grave problem, but also of a tug at consumers' hearts and minds, should already be evident. Big farmers, the other 20–30 percent of all growers, can draw on various resources unavailable to the small producers, as the case of geospatial shows.

What, more precisely, does "small farmer" mean? In Kenya, there are productive coffee farms as small as half an acre (.2 hectare), although for many growers the crop is a kind of hobby; they lose money on it. In American agriculture, "small family farms" of any type average 231 acres (93.5 hectares); the definition relies on gross income, not size of the farmland. That still makes most American coffee producers in Hawaii and Puerto Rico small farmers (note that coffee is now also grown on several farms in particular microclimates in California). At the prices fetched by Kona coffee, from Hawaii's Big Island—as much as $60 or more for a pound of roasted beans—small producers there can certainly make money. After the devastation of Hurricane Maria in the fall of 2017, it will probably take at least three years for production to recover in Puerto Rico, if it ever does.

Brazil uses the term "family farm" instead of small farm. In the country's Northeast zone, a family farm can be as large as 360 hectares, or close to 890 acres. That would be a big farm in much of the United States, let alone in France or the Netherlands. The limiting factor in the Brazilian definition of family farm is that labor must be mostly from the household.

The simplest description of a small coffee farmer entails reliance on the family above all, not on hired labor; lack of much machinery on the farm, except for possibly a pulper—more on that in a moment—and hence the necessity to sell beans that at most have gone through only the initial stages of processing.

One examination of the economy of coffee in Latin America defines small farmers as those who cultivate less than 3 hectares. A small farm may have 1,100–1,600 trees per hectare, while a medium farm of 3–20 hectares may have a density of 2,000–3,000 trees, and a large farm of more than 20 hectares may have a density of more than 3,300 trees. Labor costs drop proportionally as size goes up, the authors maintain, so that on small farms labor is 45 percent of all costs; on medium farms it is 39 percent; on large farms it is 21 percent.[27] These figures are rough guidelines, not precise statements.

Large farms can be large indeed—3,000 hectares or more. Brazil's Ipanema Company has several properties and altogether about 10 million trees, which produce 85,000 bags a year or about 31 bags per hectare.[28] The biggest coffee grower in the United States is Hawaii's Kauai Coffee Company, which farms more than 31,000 acres (1,255 hectares) with more than 4 million trees.

WOMEN IN COFFEE

The specialty coffee industry, as well as many national organizations in coffee-producing countries and international NGOs, has focused particular attention in the past few decades on women in coffee farming. Of course, women have taken the initiative in many cases by themselves. There are active all-female co-ops in Colombia, for example. Co-ops mixed by gender, for example, Musasa in Rwanda, have many active female members in important roles. This collective, which opened in 1994 with three hundred members, now has more than eighteen hundred. Many of the women are widows from the Rwandan genocide; they have gotten some part of their lives back in coffee farming and processing.[29]

Why such interest and activity regarding women? The Bill and Melinda Gates Foundation comments:

> We receive some grant proposals that do not account for gender differences and do not consider how agricultural initiatives may benefit or hinder women or men. We refer to such proposals as gender neutral. The foundation does not support these types of projects because women can be further marginalized if their concerns and needs are not explicitly factored into the program design.[30]

The nonprofit advice and aid group Root Capital uses the phrase "applying a gender lens to our work in smallholder agricultural finance." Along with books like *Half the Sky*, by Nicholas D. Kristof and Sheryl WuDunn,[31] NGOs like Root realize that economic improvement is severely hampered if women are not brought into the workforce at decent wages and if they do not have access to education. Women who work at rewarding jobs are, moreover, less likely to marry as teenagers, have fewer children, and have a better chance to get at least basic education. They will therefore be less controlled by their husbands or other male relatives. This is a chicken-and-egg question, as education and later marriage and child-bearing help women find better work in the first place.

Café Femenino, an American NGO founded in 2004, has as its mission to "Enhance the lives of women and families in the coffee-producing communities throughout the world." The foundation finds that,

> Despite ongoing progress, gender inequality, poverty and abuse continue to be rampant in many coffee production regions. Although most women coffee pro-

ducers participate in all farm activities, they have few rights and little voice when it comes to selling their coffee or making decisions on how the family income will be spent. With no control of income and very few options, these women hold out hope for a better life.[32]

Café Femenino also points out that the health of any small coffee-producing family, especially of the children, improves when women have a greater say in what goes on. The same improvement follows when women are educated. Citing a report by the World Health Organization from 2005, Femenino provided figures on domestic abuse affecting women in the Peruvian countryside: "69% of the women located in rural areas near Cusco had experienced physical or sexual violence by a partner. Additionally, only 44% of women in the department of Cusco had at least one year of secondary education."[33]

Root Capital is increasingly focusing its financial resources on enterprises that are "gender inclusive," given the hard facts that women raising coffee are less likely to have access to capital or even to join co-ops.[34] The Coffee Quality Institute (CQI), based in Portland, Oregon, began a "Partnership for Gender Equality" in 2015. Research is under way to determine what particular problems women face in several countries, to be followed by information and assistance that should enable them to improve their situation. In the announcement of the program, CQI quoted Konrad Brits, head of Britain's Falcon Coffee. "Poverty is the greatest hurdle to sustainable agriculture and the protection of bio-diversity," he said. When women in coffee cultivation are not empowered, he continued, "we cannot hope to achieve what we have to achieve" in agriculture and protection of the environment.[35]

Migration from coffee-producing areas is also of great concern to these organizations, as life for women left behind as men go to towns, or for women who also leave the countryside to move to urban areas, can be tough indeed. Helping women to have better lives on the farms is an important step toward their greater well-being, toward improving the social health of producing countries, and toward improved protection of the land itself.

Women's issues are everyone's issues. Basic problems, not just in coffee, cannot be solved if women are left behind. Female leaders I have met in the industry, for instance, Mausi Kuhl in Nicaragua and Nancy Hernandez Contreras of Honduras, are impressive for their coffee skills and managerial abilities. There is every reason to promote the abilities of half the world's population for the benefit of all. Women have a long way to go before they achieve any-thing like equality in coffee farming, or for that matter at any level in the cof-fee commodity chain and industry. But the growing attention, resources, and energy for and mostly by women in coffee have already led to some progress. We should all hope for much more.

GATHERING AND PROCESSING THE HARVEST

No matter who grows the coffee, the fruit after harvesting moves on to process-ing by a number of routes. In the leanest and least income-producing kind of coffee agriculture, farmers take their picked cherries and sell them by the side of the road or transport them to a buyer. The fruit is not processed by the farmers in any way. Such simple handling occurs with robusta in poor areas of Africa, although I have seen it with arabica in upscale Kona as well.

The cherries can be picked by hand, the practice on small farms; by people working with small power tools; or by machines on large, more or less flat farms. All these methods involve some inefficiency, either in labor or extraneous material from the trees. Not all coffee cherries, even on the same branch, ripen at the same time. Thus hand pickers may have to make four or more passes through the trees over a period of weeks to get all the ripe fruit. Workers tie baskets around their waists; they pull, with a slight twist, ripe cherries from the branches. Good pickers can make harvesting sound like strong rain as the fruit drops into their baskets. When baskets are full, workers empty them into large bags placed around the field. Eventually people will move those bags, which the moist fruit makes really heavy, on their backs or on a burro or tractor, down to a central point. Pickers are generally paid by the weight of their bags, allowing for the inevitable twigs and leaves that fall among the beans.

I have picked coffee, although only for an hour or so at a time. It's hard work. After a while, my arms ached, and I had to constantly adjust my footing to keep from sliding down the hill. Picking is not necessarily skilled labor, yet the differ-ence in the amount of cherries an experienced person can gather per hour and the amount I could harvest was dramatic. Children may of course be pickers; parents moving through the fields want to know where their kids are, preferably close by. Few farms are large or wealthy enough to have daycare. On many small family farms, the children must pitch in to make the operation viable.

In Nicaragua, I watched men who probably weighed no more than 150 pounds each carry sacks of wet coffee cherries 20 feet or so from a loading point to the bed of a pickup, which soon sank down so far that the springs were compressed against the truck frame. One man would stand and wait for two others to hoist a bag, which probably weighed more than 100 pounds, and set it on the first one's shoulders. A slap on the bag would signal to him that he could start to walk, or stagger, with his load to the truck. This part of the harvesting was carefully segregated by gender; although men, women, and children picked the coffee, only men loaded the wet sacks onto the truck. I wondered about the truck's lifespan but more about how many years a man could continue doing that kind of work. Fortunately in one sense, the harvest season lasts only two or three months. Still, migrant pickers often move up in latitude from country to country, away from the equator, as the fruit ripens, and climb in altitude as well.

Pickers relaxing after a long day at Macer Café, Marcala, Nicaragua.
Photo by Robert Thurston

In Nicaragua, a good picker could earn $5 a day in early 2016. In Costa Rica, minimum wage laws must be observed for pickers, and efficient ones can earn, according to farm employees I spoke to in early 2018, $30 to $40 per day; exceptional pickers can earn even more. The same pickers may work first in Costa Rica, then move north into Nicaragua as the harvest begins there a bit later. For the most part, working conditions are also better in Costa Rica. That country stands out in all of Latin America for standard of living, pay, and environmental protection.

After the harvest, the work on and around the trees mostly involves pruning, mulching, and generally cleaning up. All or nearly all the pickers leave. They have to save the money they have just earned and in some cases try to live on it for months or even until the next harvest.

Sometimes pickers are told just to strip all the fruit from the branches. Wearing gloves, we hope, the workers grab a branch close to the trunk and pull toward themselves, tearing everything off. This deposits ripe fruit but also unripe berries, twigs, and leaves in the baskets or on cloths spread around the bottom of the tree. Before this mess is even taken to the first processing point, the larger extraneous material should be separated. That can be done as easily as putting everything on a screen and tossing it into the air. The wind will carry leaves away, but the pickers must remove twigs and other debris by hand.

Some day, small, motorized picking machines will move up and down the steep slopes of many coffee-producing regions and harvest cherries. As early as 2008, I heard about such machines in development in Costa Rica. Getting them on line is not merely a question of reducing labor costs; the number of pickers, especially reliable and experienced ones, is already declining in some places. Costa Rican farmers have a hard time finding local pickers, so they import Nicaraguans.

So far, enough Nicas are around who can't get better jobs and who therefore pick coffee every year. But substantial government efforts are under way to boost the number of children who attend school and the number of grades they finish. The literacy rate rose from 65.7 percent of the population age 15 and over in 1995 to almost 83 percent in 2015.[36] Nicaragua's economy is growing, slowly but in recent years steadily, so there will be better jobs each year for literate people. We will see what happens with the coffee harvest in Central America in the next few decades—if global warming does not destroy much of the crop first.

The most extreme case of a labor shortage in coffee is Hawaii, where Mexicans are flown in to some farms to gather the fruit. Among Brazilian producers, some have "solved" their labor issues through neo-slavery; poor men desperate for work are lured to farms with promises of good pay. Once there, owners and local police seize their identification documents and hold the men on the farms, by force if necessary.[37] Needless to say, working and living conditions on such farms are miserable. But the gist of advice from Catholic Relief Services, which wrote the main report on Brazilian coffee slavery, is don't turn away from Brazilian coffee. Instead, pay attention to where exactly the coffee comes from. Don't hesitate to ask your local coffee store about that. Meanwhile, I can testify that the large Brazilian farms I saw don't use slaves and do provide protective gear for their workers. But I did not go deep into the countryside.

Another way of picking is to use gas-powered machines about the size of a grass trimmer. On one common type, the business end has a pair of shears that close around a branch; pickers then pull everything on that limb toward themselves, allowing it all to fall onto a cloth. Once more, much of the collected material is not usable coffee, and the technique is still labor intensive.

Small farming versus big farming is not only a question of who does the work on what land or of labor versus capital, but also of topography. Where the land is relatively flat, large machines can be used. That possibility draws capital to a region, making big farms more feasible.

On Kauai Coffee's farm and on other capital-intensive operations, especially in Brazil, large and clumsy machines with an opening in the center crawl slowly over rows of trees at harvest time. The center cavity is fitted with nylon or fiberglass wands that spin rapidly and knock material off the branches into a pan. The machine may have the capacity to store all the cherries and debris for a while, or it may have a device that sucks the collected material up through a tube and over the trees to a truck moving in tandem between the rows of plants.

However the cherries are gathered, initial sorting—beyond using the wind's help—can be as simple as pouring everything collected onto screens that allow the coffee fruit to fall through but catch larger material like twigs. Then the coffee may be further sorted in water tanks, the heavier and riper beans falling to the bottom while the unripe berries float along on the top and can be easily removed. On small African farms, this may be done by pouring the cherries into buckets of water and removing the unripe ones by hand. Yet this same painstaking practice can also be found on Kona farms.

At this point, another kind of hand sorting is also done in some places, notably in Africa. Workers, mostly women, pick out unripe cherries spread out on tables, the ground, or on a moving belt. Although this kind of labor is hard, at least the people are usually in shade and can socialize as they work and take breaks together.

Once the fruit is off the tree, the coffee can be wet processed, dry processed, or handled in a combination of the two. In wet processing, which takes place in a wet mill (*beneficio* in Spanish), also called a micromill, the fruit is first pulped. The cherries are fed by gravity into a machine, large or small, hand or fuel-powered. Here, usually with the help of flowing water, a rotating drum presses the fruit against a screen, forcing the skin and part of the mucilage through and away from the beans, which are moved down and out of the machine. Next the beans slide into water tanks for twelve to twenty-four hours, during which the action of the water and of microorganisms eats away at the remaining mucilage. In the best practices, the water will be filtered and used again, at least for irrigation.

Demucilating machines, which rub the beans against each other, are at work in some well-funded wet mills. In any event, fermentation now takes place. The microorganisms that consume mucilage, among them a variety of *E. coli*, produce ethanol as they act, change the structure of sugars in the beans, and bring the acidity (pH level here; we will soon hear about another use of the word *acidity* concerning coffee) to around 4.0. Too low or too high a pH at this point will produce unpleasant flavors in the cup—sour, bitter, or rancid. Small farmers may develop a feel for level of acidity as they touch beans in water tanks; larger producers use test equipment. After some time in water or a demucilating machine, the beans may dry for a day or two on the farm on patios or African drying racks, screens set up on legs. These racks can now be found around the world on small farms. The humidity (water content) of the beans should drop to about 12–15 percent at this point.

At first sniff, the air around a wet mill of even medium size at harvest time is sickly sweet, an unforgettable and almost overpowering odor. But the nose quickly adjusts, and the clanking and banging noises of the machinery become a kind of rhythm that, we understand, is essential to coffee's journey. And, although there may be temporary piles of organic debris at a wet mill, it should essentially be clean. Dirt and waste, including coffee cherries, skins, or mucilage stuck to basins or equipment, are also enemies of cup quality. Everything that gets wet must be cleaned regularly. The workers are soon dirty, but not the way they would be on a pig farm or an old-style factory. Since the temperature is mild, working conditions at micromills are usually tolerable, except for the back-breaking job in some cases of carrying sacks of wet cherries up steps to feed into the pulper.

Dry processing, on the other hand, may not even begin with picking the cherries. Some can be left on the trees until they are well fermented, which with the proper varieties can produce especially sweet coffee. With the wrong kind of coffee, however, the outcome may be overfermentation and nasty tastes in the cup like iodine or phenols. For the most part, dry processing does start with picked beans but forgoes quick pulping. Instead, the newly harvested cherries are left in their skins and spread on patios to dry. Again, microorganisms go to work on the fruit, and the sun dries out some mucilage. When the managers think that proper pH and humidity levels have been reached, the skins and any remaining mucilage are removed by machine. Beans handled in this way are called "naturals."

A middle way involves pulped or semipulped naturals. The skin and some mucilage are removed in the same fashion as in the beginning of wet treatment. Then, with a good deal of mucilage remaining over the beans, they are spread out to dry. Also called honey coffee, in the view of many growers this method imparts more sweetness to the cup.

Good coffee should have some natural sweetness, not bitterness. But sometimes I think that consumers widely believe that coffee will always be bitter and then, no surprise, discover that taste in what is really an excellent cup. Try sipping a fine cup of coffee before adding any milk or sugar to it. In the early English coffeehouses of the seventeenth and eighteenth centuries, beans—probably often already stale—were ground and tossed into iron kettles, followed by water. The coffee then boiled or stayed close to the boil for hours. No wonder the English put milk and sugar into their drinks. Be kind to yourself and to good coffee, and try to get away from the milk, which adds a good deal of sweetness by itself, not to mention sugar and its calories.

❧

Finally, there is a process which has been delicately described as "intestinal fermentation."[38] Animals eat coffee cherries, partially digest them, and excrete beans. Few creatures will eat ripe berries; the main gourmand is the civet cat, about the size of a large house cat, which lives in Indonesia. In Brazil the jacu bird consumes cherries, while apparently a few African elephants also indulge. Someone must come along to sort out the poop and remove the coffee beans. The best-known product of this type is called Kopi Luwak. At $11.25 an ounce in one ad, or $180 to $300 a pound, "wild, organic civet coffee" is pricey indeed. But few people seem to think it's any good, and it is never rated high. Recently some Indonesians, not being stupid, have captured civet cats, caged them, and fed them coffee cherries. The major point of all this seems to be that anyone who has tried poop coffee can brag about it to others.

No particular rules determine which varieties of coffee are better as wet processed, dry processed, or semipulped. Water limitations dictate the dry method in some locales, while the tradition of wet processing or "washed" coffee rules in much of Latin America. But experiments go on all the time, as farmers seek to save water and to bring out the best flavors of their beans. For example, Ethiopian Yirgacheffe—referring to a region of the country rather than to specific varieties—which is often characterized as having blueberry notes in the cup, may be processed in different ways. A single farm may use several methods.

Indian "monsooned coffee," typically from the Malabar coast, may be left uncovered as cherry, allowing the annual wind and rain to sweep over it for twelve to sixteen weeks. Subjecting the cherries to nature in this way can produce a "potpourri of caramel, dark chocolate, nuts, pipe tobacco, earthy, and a hint of spice."[39] At any rate, that is an ideal description of how monsooned beans taste in the cup.

Regardless of how the beans reach a desired level of humidity and acidity, they usually go next to a "dry" mill, located at a lower altitude to take advantage of stronger sunlight. At this point, the mill supervisors check the beans for defects. By inserting a long concave knife into the jute bags, beans can be drawn out for a quick look. Among defects are: beans damaged by insects, frost, or overfermentation (black beans); clearly unripe beans; or broken ones. Iron deficiency in the soil can result in yellowish beans that in the cup will have a grassy or woody flavor. Foreign matter, usually small twigs or stones, but sometimes bullets and even teeth, is a serious defect. If coffee cherries or beans covered with parchment make it through processing to end up in bags with green coffee, those are also defects. Any irregular edge can be an especially hospitable site for fungus. Once in a while someone will put a can of gasoline next to coffee beans in the back of a pickup on its way to the dry mill. When the odor of gas gets into beans, they are ruined forever. Farmers may work hard from harvest to harvest, only to find that their beans are worthless at the next stage.

In a complex scoring system for green coffee, defects are noted as primary, "full" and "partial," and "secondary." Generally, in specialty coffee no more than five full defects per 350 grams (about 12.34 ounces) are allowed in green coffee for export. One black bean is one full defect, for example, while it takes five broken or chipped beans to make one full defect. Severe insect damage, usually from broca, registers as five full defects by itself.

Beans that make it to a dry mill are free of mucilage. They are still covered with a parchment layer and are called, for short, parchment. Underneath that layer is silverskin. In any capital-intensive operation, the beans may first be fed

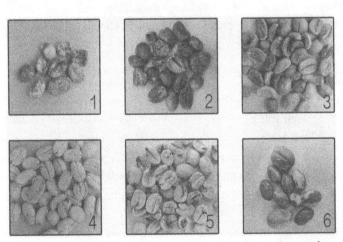

Samples of defects found during or after processing. Number 1: damage from fungus; 2: black beans, way overfermented; 3: immature beans; 4: beans still covered in parchment; 5: beans damaged by broca; note the small holes left by the insects; 6: cherries that somehow made it through all steps of processing.
Samples courtesy of the IHCAFE research station at San Pedro Sula, Honduras. Arrangement and labels by Lara Thurston, photos by Robert Thurston

into mechanical density sorters, sometimes called pre-cleaners, that are raised and slanted beds with screens that shake the beans and move them slowly down the slope of the machine. A partial or separate top screen with fairly large holes lets beans through but catches bigger material such as leaves and twigs. Light and less dense beans move to the lower side of the slanted table and are drawn off into a channel. Denser, higher quality beans move to the upper third of the table and are also drawn off or simply slide down and out of the machine. This is a simple way of starting to grade the coffee; denser beans are generally better. At the same time, the screens sort the beans by size. The largest usual screen size is number 20, 7.94 mm (think of almost eight dimes in a stack) in diameter; number 12 is usually smallest, at 4.76 mm. The point is more to ensure that the beans are even in size, so that in roasting, they will absorb heat evenly. A destoner may also be used at this juncture; again, the denser and heavier stones will move to the top of a slanted bed, while coffee will move down and out.

The next step at the dry mill is, naturally, to further dry the beans, which ideally have been separated by organic/conventional, by certification scheme, if any, and by farm, and even by particular fields on farms. The beans are spread out on patios in the sun for ten to fifteen days. To prevent mold from developing, the coffee must be raked each day. This stage should occur in a dry season; if it does rain, workers must quickly cover the coffee. Raking also serves to keep the temperature of the drying coffee from getting too high. If that happens, the parchment layer can crack or the beans may actually toast, leading to insolvable problems in roasting.

Small farms unable to afford concrete may dry coffee directly on dirt. With more capital but less area to cover, an old technique works well: plastic or even glass canopies that can be rolled over the beans if it rains. Finally, well-financed operations may use large dryers, like a clothes dryer but much bigger. The advantages are control over drying and shortening the time needed to dry the beans.

Drying, especially on patios, can't be too fast, or the moisture content in the beans will become uneven. That in turn can lead to serious problems when the parchment coffee is stored. Some of the beans might then be susceptible to fungus, and beans with varying internal moisture will not roast evenly.

Parchment is kept in jute or plastic sacks piled high in warehouses. It used to be common to store beans this way for years; more recently, the finest coffees are warehoused only for short periods, then are milled to remove the parchment and

Workers raking coffee at Macer Coffee's dry mill, Matagalpa, Nicaragua.
Photo by Robert Thurston

shipped to roasters within a few months of harvesting. Even where the temperature and humidity in storage remain steady, changes in the chemical structure of
the beans can occur. They are still living organisms that must respire. To prevent undesirable changes in the chemistry of the beans, they must be stored in
a dormant state, and their moisture content should be ideally held at 12 percent
for arabica. Defects can also be induced at the wet or dry mill, for instance, in
beans crushed or nipped by pulpers. Beans dried at too high a temperature can
crystallize, producing a cup with grassy notes.

As parchment coffee, arabica should be held back for some ten days before
hulling. "Dry" or "ball" cherry, which has been dry processed, can be stored for
longer periods, as the skin protects the bean. Storage structures need to be well
ventilated; otherwise, temperature can rise in the beans. Even in well-managed
storehouses, an array of pests can attack the beans. Once in a consuming country, coffee beans may be stored again in importers' warehouses, preferably in
climate-controlled rooms.

Beans older than one year are called past crop and are not as desirable as more freshly processed beans. Past crop coffee might still be very good, but it often loses some subtle flavor notes, assuming that the coffee was of superior quality to begin with.

Parchment coffee must be hulled (milled), optimally shortly before shipping. Machines, set for the size of the beans to be milled, use mechanical arms or rub the beans against each other to remove the parchment. Here, too, the beans can be damaged, while temperature control is critical. The beans must also not be too moist, which can jam the huller. In the same or a separate machine, the coffee is polished to remove almost all of the silverskin, although some inevitably remains in the central crack of each bean. What is left blows off in roasting as chaff.

The beans should now be screened once more for size. Uniform density and color are the goals at this point, again to make roasting uniform. Grading machines, called gravity separators or densimetric tables, shake a slanted, perforated bed and blow air from below through the vibrating beans, lifting the lighter and less worthy ones above the table and down the slope. These devices can also have screens to sort by bean size. Color sorters are also used at this point on capital-intensive operations. These machines detect off-color beans and blow them out of the main flow with puffs of air. Where labor is cheap, all of these sorting techniques are done by hand. However, some particularly picky customers may ask for a final hand sorting, as I have seen in Colombia.

Now the coffee is bagged. The jute, with or without plastic inserts, may be sewn shut by machine or by hand. When enough bags are ready, they are trucked to a port and loaded into containers—although experiments are under way to load unbagged green coffee directly into containers lined with plastic.

After all this manipulation in a producing country and more to come where the coffee is prepared as beverages, 100 pounds of coffee cherries might return 12–15 pounds of roasted coffee. Some of the loss is water. The rest of the removed material—skins, mucilage, and defective beans—can be composted; with the help of California red worms, a useful mulch/fertilizer results in several weeks. This "vermicomposting" produces castings, or worm fecal material, fine particles that contain nutrients much more easily used by plants than untreated waste. The level of phosphorus, for instance, nearly doubles when worms get to work. They also break down caffeine, which many plants cannot tolerate. Enterprising farmers also raise and sell worms, not just to other coffee producers but to operations like fish farms. Vermicompost can be bagged and used in country or exported. Worms and the bacteria that assist them are an inexpensive way to boost farmers' efficiency and income.

THE COST OF COFFEE THROUGH THE SUPPLY CHAIN

The 2006 film *Black Gold*, repeating an old claim about prices, announced that coffee costs $3.00 a cup in a big Western city but that farmers make $3.00 a day. Even if this notion were true, is not especially useful. First, what does "day" mean for a farmer, especially a poor one? A day can be sixteen hours at critical moments like harvesting, or it can be two hours in a slack season. The whole family works at certain times but not at others. Second, coffee farmers, like others, are not paid by the day. They take in money when they sell their crops after a harvest. Nor does the formula take into account the many costs involved in the process of cupping and buying coffee alone. Farmers may get nothing at all for their coffee if the beans have been ruined, or they may have excellent coffee that commands a good price even at the farm gate, where the farmers actually receive money, as opposed to payments to a co-op, an exporter, importer, roaster, or café owner.

Some coffees fetch extremely high prices. One Colombian coffee, green and still in the country, sold in a special auction in early 2017 for $31 per pound. As roasted coffee, it would probably retail in a consuming country for twice that price. The Honduran coffee that won that country's Cup of Excellence competition in 2017 sold for $126.50 per pound. One lot of 'Gesha' coffee from the revered farm La Esmeralda in Boquete, Panama, sold in the same year at the farm's annual online auction for $601 per pound. I have seen it for sale for $55 a cup. It is exquisite coffee, with complex floral, fruit, and cocoa flavors. Yet even La Esmeralda's price for green coffee pales beside a reported figure of $5,001.50 per kilogram (approximately $2,273 per pound) recently paid by the company Green Hills. The coffee is from the 'José Alfredo Gesha Series', grown at Ninety Plus Gesha Estates in Panama. The farm promises that "José Alfredo fermentation style delivers unprecedented complexity in the cup and promises an expanded future of the mind-boggling taste experiences displayed in this exciting series."[40] Such verbiage and this kind of money have nothing to do with rational decision-making; presumably, someone needs the kind of status that paying these prices might confer in some minds.

Few in the coffee industry even dream of living in that kind of universe. Small producers are fortunate to get a few dollars per pound. They must first somehow make enough money to survive between payments for harvested coffee. Because having land provides some prestige and solidity to life—small farmers are not rootless—and because of the intangible value of living close to the earth in a beautiful place, keeping the farm going almost "no matter what" is extremely important to many cultivators. Preserving the quality of the land is a close third priority, since exhausted soil precludes continued agriculture.

Small farmers do not realize much of the value added to coffee as it progresses from fields to beverage. Of course, someone working on a coffee farm in Ethiopia does not pay for heat, light, rent, labor, advertising, and so on in Manhattan. The coffee must fetch a lot more money per pound in New York or London than it does at the farm gate.

To see how and why the cost of coffee changes as it goes through the supply chain, I will use my own roastery.

- I recently paid $4 per pound for green Burundi coffee, which is pretty good stuff.
- $1.50 is what I charge for an 8-ounce cup of regular, brewed coffee. To make that cup, I use, as noted, about 15 grams of ground coffee, or .033 of a pound.
- One pound of coffee makes about 30 cups.
- $45 per pound is therefore the value of my coffee now.

This may look sweet for me. But, taking a month almost at random, October 2016, my cost for green coffee was about 21 percent of my total expenses. I barely spent more for coffee than for rent. Wages cost me three times as much as the green coffee did. Therefore my $1.50 price per 8-ounce cup must cover various other expenses as well.

Looking back to Burundi, we see that about $1.12 per pound of green coffee was the premium farm gate price that one organization, Crop to Cup (C2C), paid to the Buhorwa group of producers in 2010, the last year for which detailed

Coffee Prices Through the Supply Chain

Step	Value
Coffee Cherry	$1.12
Transport	$0.34
Washing	$0.57
Exporter Markup	$0.55
Financing	$0.42
Importer Markup	$1.00
Roasted Wholesale Markup	$9.00
Roasted Retail Markup	$6.00
Total	$19.00

■ Coffee Cherry ■ Transport ■ Washing ■ Exporter Markup
■ Financing ■ Importer Markup ▨ Roasted Wholesale Markup ▨ Roasted Retail Markup

$0.00 $5.00 $10.00 $15.00 $20.00

The price of a pound of Burundi coffee goes up at each stage in the commodity chain. The numbers in the right-hand column show how the value of the coffee changes at each point.
Chart by Lara Thurston

data are available. But C2C bought coffee cherry, not green coffee, from the farmers. The company had to calculate for loss of weight in processing to get the $1.12 amount for green coffee. Then it cost about .57/lb. to have the coffee washed at a station and later milled. Another .34/lb. covered transportation and other requirements to get the coffee to a port in Tanzania. That part of the total is really expensive; but Burundi is landlocked and its infrastructure is poor. C2C finally calculated its costs for the coffee onboard a ship, outside of U.S. customs (there is no import duty on coffee) at $2.57/lb.[41]

There the trail from C2C runs out, but 3.00 will serve as a rough estimate of the value per pound once the coffee entered the U.S., reached a storage destination, and further charges, for example, financing, were figured in.

Again, what the importer charged me was $4.00 a pound, which seems reasonable given the other expenses involved for that stage: utilities, rent, general and administrative, and especially labor. The price for green coffee around the level of the Burundi—in the high 80s (we will get to the scale in a few pages), I would say—has not increased since 2011.

I sold a 12-ounce bag (the standard size in the industry for roasted coffee) of the Burundi for $9.75 wholesale and $14.25 retail (per pound, $13 wholesale and $19 retail).

The $1.12 that our Burundi farmers received at the farm gate thus swelled, in a more or less normal course of events largely determined by market forces and the cost of doing business, to the nominal value of $30 per pound in beverages, or 26 times greater. The bagged coffee I sold rose in value 17 times for retail, less for wholesale.

Because of all my costs, I am not yet getting rich selling coffee this way. For the most part, no one is making a big profit in the commodity chain, although millions of sales—especially of coffee heavily charged with milk, as in lattes and cappuccinos—can result in billions in net revenue for a company like Starbucks.

How, in this matrix of price, productivity, value added, and costs at each stage, can anyone determine what is social justice? Certainly the $1.12 per pound of harvested coffee that Burundi farmers received in 2010 did not make them well off. Back in the coffee crisis, the years 2002–2004, farmers were often not getting enough for their crops to cover their expenses. It may have required then, at a very rough estimate, an average of $.70 around the world to produce a pound of arabica coffee. But to bring the Burundi coffee to a consuming country, roast it, and make it into liquor, cost a lot.

In another disturbing scenario, farmers in Uganda went to the side of the road in 2002 and sold their sun-dried robusta to middlemen for about 6.3 U.S. cents a pound. By the time it reached the exporter, after further processing and storage, the coffee was worth some 12 cents per pound. Ultimately, the coffee sold as soluble (instant) in jars in British grocery stores for $12 a pound, nearly 20 times its worth in Uganda. Is that social injustice, brutal economics, or both? The problems for the Ugandan producers were that their coffee was of low quality and that their contribution to the value chain was small compared to everything else needed to bring the soluble to a point of sale. Nevertheless, the company involved in this case, Nestlé, made as much as 26 to 30 percent profit on its sales of instant in 2002, according to some analysts.[42]

More recently, midgrade arabica grown in Brazil has been estimated to cost on average $1.26 to produce, considering labor, capital costs, fertilizer, and so on.[43] Nicaraguan farmers told me in 2016 that $1.50 per pound of arabica was a useful rule of thumb for production costs in that country. This is well below the break-even point of $2.50 per pound given above. At any rate, there is no such thing as a global average cost of production.

The international "price" of coffee mentioned in many articles refers to dollars per 100 pounds of green coffee on the New York exchange, now called ICE. This figure, often referred to as the benchmark price for coffee, is called the Coffee C® price. It relates to "deliverable growths" due to arrive at any of several major ports—New York, Hamburg, and Barcelona among them—on scheduled dates in the next few months. The name of the game is futures; the price is for delivery on a future date, noted first in dollars per 100 pounds.

The "deliverable growths," an unappealing name for green coffee, takes into account beans from a range of producing countries and gives them a kind of general rating. Arabica beans from Mexico, El Salvador, Guatemala, Costa Rica, Nicaragua, Kenya, Papua New Guinea, Panama, Tanzania, Uganda, Honduras, and Peru are all "at par" on ICE. Colombians, considered generally better in this scheme, receive a "400 [basis] point premium." Burundi, Rwanda, Venezuela, and India come in at a 100 point discount, the Dominican Republic and Ecuador at a 400 point discount, and Brazil at 600 points lower.[44]

Points are not the same as percentages; 1 basis point is .01 percent; 100 basis points equals 1 percent. This system is used to avoid the ambiguity in saying that something increased in value by, for example, 10 percent. Does that mean that an item that did cost $14 now costs $15.40 (14 plus .10 times 14, or $1.40 more, to add up to $15.40)? Or does an increase of 10 percent mean that the item went up to $14.10? To illustrate, let's say that the C price today is $140 per 100 pounds. With their point differential, Colombians would fetch $144. Burundi, Rwanda, Venezuela, and India come in at a 100 point discount, or at $139. The Dominican and Ecuadorian beans are at a 400 point discount ($136) and Brazilians are 600 points lower ($134).

These values are not arbitrary, as Brazil produces a huge amount of really ordinary arabica. But Brazil also exports excellent coffee, which can compete with the best Colombians. I have had wonderful Burundi coffee, but I have tried beans from Papua New Guinea that I did not care for and that had numerous small stones, exactly the size of the beans, in each bag. Note that Ethiopia is not on the list, as coffee from there can vary tremendously in quality, and because in recent years the country has endured some serious marketing and labeling problems. Vietnam is not listed either, because its production is largely robusta.

The "contract size" for arabica coffee futures is 37,500 pounds, which excludes carefully tended, picked, and processed micro-lots. While commodity coffee, as contrasted to specialty coffee, remains a fairly vague term, the C market deals with bulk shipments. I think of coffee sold there as pretty good but not great.

The robusta exchange, also handled by ICE, is quite different. Not only are the prices lower, the deliverable growths can come from anywhere and be shipped anywhere. It's not that no one cares; rather, robusta is often judged less by quality than by its usefulness in blends or soluble.

Arabica reached an all-time high on the C market of 339.86 per 100 pounds in April of 1977 and a record low of 42.50 in October of 2001.[45] In 2011 the C price went as high as 311, but it has not reached that level since. To take a recent example, for delivery in May of 2017, the C figure was (switching to dollars per pound) between $1.39 and $1.41. The price had fallen from $1.76 in November 2016; that difference could make or break many coffee traders. Various factors can send the price up or down—for example, a drought in Brazil, a flood in Vietnam, or a bumper crop in Colombia. This is a highly volatile game.

These fluctuations do not immediately affect farmers' income, as they have usually either sold their beans to a middleman at harvest time, or, at high levels

TWO BROTHERS GROWING COFFEE

In the summer of 2017, I met Milton and Alexi Moreno on their adjoining farms above Peña Blanca, Honduras. Having switched to high-end coffee—called "specialty" in Honduras—they have started to sell much more coffee. In 2015/16, they sold 12 bags; in 2016/17, they sold 38 bags. They had small but comfortable houses with disc TV antennas, good cell phone service, and new coffee drying shelters they built themselves. The only big problem they faced was the terrible road down to processing facilities. But all in all, they were happy and optimistic about the future.

of quality, they have signed yearly contracts to deliver a certain amount of beans processed to a certain point. It is the traders—beans may change hands many times before they reach a roaster—who take the big gains or losses as ownership of the coffee changes. Often traders don't even see the coffee they buy and sell, much as people who own stock don't see the lightbulbs or cars a company makes.

Nonetheless, the coffee C price remains important for farmers' income. Coffee buyers looking for beans at their preferred quality level are keenly aware of the C price and will adjust their offers accordingly. The buyers must judge whether the coffee they "cup"—more on that in a moment—is above or below the exchange-grade beans in quality. Many contracts are tied to the C price. Farmers, as they gain access to global communications, are also increasingly more aware of Coffee C. What they can do about it is another matter.

CERTIFICATION PROGRAMS: BENEFITS AND DRAWBACKS

Since the C price fluctuates and can be well below the cost of production for many farmers, various organizations have adopted certification schemes that aim to boost the amount farmers get for their coffee while providing money to improve their lives and the environment. Together, these plans refer to "ethical" coffees, a nice claim to the moral high ground. Organic is the best-known of these certifications. Second in name recognition is Fair Trade, which covers both organic and nonorganic coffee. Lesser known but gaining in recognition is Rainforest Alliance. Other programs include Utz (now merged with Rainforest), Starbucks' Coffee and Farmer Equity Practices (C.A.F.E.), and (Smithsonian) Bird Friendly®.

The Fair Trade idea began in 1988 in the Netherlands with a label taken from a famous Dutch novel by Multatuli, *Max Havelaar: Or the Coffee Auctions of the Dutch Trading Company*, published in 1860. The book, set in the Dutch East Indies (now largely Indonesia) in the 1840s, is still a classic in the Netherlands and is very much worth reading. It unveiled the extremely nasty practices of the Dutch East India Company as it extorted coffee and other products from Indonesians. The VOC, to use its Dutch initials, left local nobles in place and merely asked them to deliver to the colonial authorities a certain amount of food, which was squeezed in turn from the peasants. Failure to comply could bring a punitive visit from the Dutch army. Especially valuable were items for export back to Europe or the U.S. Coffee grew well in the East Indies and was a major part of the VOC's list. As Multatuli wrote, the result of taking

> food on board the ships which are being laden with the harvests that make Holland rich! [was]
>
> *Famine?* In rich, fertile, blessed Java—*famine?* Yes, reader. Only a few years ago, whole districts died of starvation. Mothers offered their children for sale to obtain food. Mothers ate their children . . .
>
> But then the Motherland [the Netherlands] took a hand in the matter. The Dutch government forbade pushing food collection "to the point of causing famine."[46]

The situation for East Indians improved somewhat, but the burden of colonial rule remained heavy.

After the Dutch lost almost all of their overseas possessions following World War II, they could feel guilty about what they had done abroad. Max Havelaar coffee was ultimately born in the Netherlands as the first Fair Trade brand. The FT idea and groups to promote it soon spread to all the developed countries and became the Fair Trade Labeling Organisations (FLO). Its contracts set a floor price the buyer pays for coffee purchased FOB (free on board), loaded onto a ship after all processing fees and export duties, if any, have been paid by the seller. The FOB price is quite different from the farm gate price; many expenses can be incurred in getting coffee from the farm onto a ship. Adjusted upward in 2011, the FT minimum price per pound of washed arabica became $1.40, for naturals $1.35, and for organic an additional 30 cents. The FT "community development premium" also increased in 2011, from 20 to 30 cents a pound. That premium is supposed to be used for projects like schools, clean water, infrastructure, or environmental improvements.

The total paid for FT coffee can go higher than these minimums but not lower. In a high C market, growers can usually get more than the floor price. Yet even in that situation, FT contracts provide stability for farmers and can make it easier for them to get loans at reasonable interest.

Fair Trade USA, which used to be called TransFair, left the FLO in 2012. The dispute arose over whether FT should cover farms of any size or should limit its contracts to its traditional clients, small growers. The Americans felt that it did not make sense to exclude large operations, as many workers on them might also benefit from FT, while the Europeans in particular believed in a kind of purity and commitment to the little guys.

Rainforest Alliance (RA), founded in 1995, aims for continuous progress toward sustainability and improvement in the lives of farmers. It concentrates on keeping the land green or adding to green space, although it too promises a better life for farmers. Thus part of a certified farm can be in coffee cultivated under full sun; to compensate, as it were, for that kind of agriculture, another part of the same farm must be forest or waterway. In 2017, RA merged with Utz Certified, which used to be Utz Kapeh (a Mayan word for coffee). Utz assesses agricultural practices but has concentrated on conditions for workers. Here, too, there is no set premium, but producers can usually expect to get six cents or more per pound than conventional beans fetch.

As RA's efforts gained momentum, the Sustainable Agriculture Network (SAN) arose from the parent organization in 1998. SAN standards are strict regarding nonconversion of forest land to agriculture, and they list 150 substances prohibited in farming, as well as an additional 170 that can be applied only under tight controls. A farm has to achieve a minimum score on the overall requirements to be certified and has to show improvement year by year. RA/Utz does not set a minimum price for coffee but avers that its certification helps producers get more for their crop, usually 5 to 10 cents a pound. The organization claims that farmers' income goes up significantly using their approved methods, for example, in Colombia by 150 percent.[47] To date, about one million farms meet the standards.

(Smithsonian) Bird Friendly® coffee is largely about shade. A minimum of 40 percent of the arable land must be shaded, and the canopy must be at least 12 meters high, with native trees dominating among all trees on the land. The coffee must also be certified organic. There is no fee for bird friendly certification, but of course the organic verification must be paid. Importers of this coffee pay $100 a year for the privilege, and roasters pay 25 cents a pound. That money mostly goes back to farmers for improvements in the environment and conditions for workers.

The focus of Starbucks' certification is on raising wages for workers, abolishing child labor, improving worker safety, and devising ways to reduce environmental impact. In May of 2015, Starbucks reported that 99 percent of its coffee imports into consuming countries either met C.A.F.E. practices or was FT and hence "ethically sourced."[48] By 2017, the company had also put some $70 million (Is that a lot or a drop in the bucket, given global profits?) into "collaborative farmer programs and activities," including help with environmental issues.[49] It is difficult to get an independent assessment of Starbucks' efforts. Nestlé also gives money and advice back to farmers.

Much criticism of certification schemes has arisen over the years. FT has borne the brunt of this opposition. It may work well for farmers when the C price is very low, but when it is high, growers have no incentive to sell at the FT minimum. If they have signed FT contracts for a low price, they may renege on the terms and sell to a higher bidder who appears at the farm gate or a co-op office. Social premiums paid to co-ops may go for extra office space or lab improvements, not directly to the farmers. Benefits from lab work can certainly reach down to the farmers, but meanwhile the lives of the small growers improve slowly if at all. Migratory pickers are not landowners or members of co-ops and so benefit from FT contracts only when farmers can afford to pay them more. Meanwhile, an array of national coffee organizations has stepped up to help small farmers.[50]

More disturbing is the problem that FT may keep people in coffee agriculture who should, at least in an economic sense, be doing something else. Although the program continues to grow, in 2015 involving 445 producing organizations and 812,500 farmers and workers, it is now clear that many of them, perhaps most, cannot survive economically in the long run. A study sponsored by Fair Trade USA and Cornell University shows that even if farmers can generate enough income to stay in business each year, they do not earn enough to cover long-term costs like replacement of tractors or motors for small processing equipment. Moreover, the study provided no calculations of the ultimate cost on family farms of keeping children out of school to work with coffee.[51] If there is a way forward for small FT growers, it will likely be through increased production and higher quality, bringing in more money regardless of whether producers sign FT contracts or not. But increased production is a goal nearly everywhere, and if it goes up and consumption does not keep pace, the price of all but the best, most-sought-after coffee will go down.

Direct trade—purchases by roasting companies at the farm gate—used to enjoy a high reputation in specialty coffee. By eliminating middlemen, it could offer farmers more income as well as incentives to improve crop quality. But lately the idea has become so diluted—even Target stores brag that their coffee is "direct trade," although they don't say from where—that it has lost its previous luster. Nonetheless, when it's possible to know that a farmer is getting more money, and more directly, for good beans, direct trade remains important.

Producing countries do offer value added in the form of high-quality coffee-processing equipment manufactured in Latin America. That industry provides a variety of decent jobs and keeps money inside the region. In particular, Pinhalense, based in Brazil but now global, makes high-quality pulpers and other machinery.

CUPPING (RATING AND PURCHASING DECISIONS)

Coffee is rated on a 100-point scale borrowed from the wine industry. Eighty points is considered the minimum for export; below that figure, the coffee is considered "fair, poor," and finally, at below 70, "not recommended." On the high side, 80–84 is "good," 85–89 "very good," 90–94 "outstanding," and 95–100 "exceptional."[52]

After many years of trial and error and a search for standard methods, a precise protocol for rating coffee was developed by the Specialty Coffee Association of America (SCAA), which recently merged with the Speciality Coffee Association of Europe (SCAE) to form the Specialty Coffee Association (SCA). Other protocols are offered by private companies. Cuppers, those hardy men and women who taste coffee where it is grown, look for quality in several categories: fragrance of the freshly ground coffee; aroma of freshly brewed coffee; acidity, here meaning sparkle on the tongue, as in sparkling wine; body or mouthfeel, as in whole milk versus skim milk; and finish, as in the way good red wine or scotch lingers in the mouth and produces flavors not immediately apparent in drinking the beverage. Up to 10 points can be awarded for each of these categories. Cuppers then add a number, up to 50, for a sense of overall flavor. When cuppers are carefully trained, especially those who have earned the coveted title Q grader from the Coffee Quality Institute, they usually come close to each other in their final scores for coffees.

Cuppers should not be at all ill and should never taste coffee when their noses are stuffy. After all, so much of taste is really assessed by our noses. Even the glasses or ceramic cups used must be the same everywhere. The size of the cupping room and the table on which samples are placed have standard parameters.

Almost all cupping is blind; the samples are numbered. No one wants an idea of what the coffee should be to interfere with the actual tasting. Usually several coffees are cupped at the same time, so that the cuppers can compare them. Big farms and many dry mills have their own cupping rooms. It is here that buyers decide which coffees to purchase.

First the coffee is roasted to the correct, medium darkness; then it usually rests for a day before cupping. When everyone is in place, the coffee is ground and the correct amount is poured into glasses or cups. The cuppers sniff the dry grounds and make notes, usually with at least a preliminary number, 0 to 10, for fragrance. Then the right amount of water, which must not have too much or too little mineral content, and is just off the boil, is poured onto the grounds. This produces a crust of coffee grounds at the top of the glass. After a few minutes, the cuppers break the crust with spoons, which may be favorite tools belonging to individual cuppers and carried from farm to farm. As the crust is broken and again later, the cuppers sniff the aroma of the brewed coffee. Again they make notes and write down a score.

Then comes the slurp, which can sound quite different from country to country; it can be on the dainty side or a big snort. The cuppers take a bit of coffee in their spoons and suck it sharply, so that very fine droplets hit the roof of their mouths, where the nasal receptors can absorb the taste. The cuppers assess mouthfeel and think about overall flavor. They let the coffee linger in their mouths for a few moments to judge the finish. But they don't drink the coffee; their caffeine intake has to be limited. Cuppers spit after every taste, into cups or spittoons, then dip their spoons into glasses of hot water, then start again on the same or another glass of coffee. They may come back to the same coffee several times and note changes in several categories, especially flavor, as the brew cools. As all this goes on, cuppers don't talk to each other.

Here's a home or coffee shop experiment: take a cup of regular, brewed (drip, pour-over) coffee of good quality. Don't add anything to it. Sip it when you first get it. Then let it sit for at least an hour—but remember that it's not nice to be a

"camper," using the industry term, who lingers in a café for a long time and orders little or nothing. See if different flavors don't emerge in the coffee as it cools. Once I heard a talk by a coffee pro who said that she loved to make a cup when she got to work at 9 a.m. but let it sit, untouched, until noon. Any way you do it, this flavor test is one way of determining whether the coffee in front of you is really special. If no new flavors appear as it cools, it isn't all that great. In many fine coffees, chocolate notes in particular will become more pronounced over time.

Having written down their sensations and scored the coffees in front of them, the cuppers decide which beans to buy. Once in a while it happens that the coffee they receive at importers or roasteries doesn't taste the same as what they had in the field. That may be due to changes in the beans during shipment; less rarely, suppliers in producing countries have switched the beans and sent something inferior. Not nice, and not likely to lead to future deals.

CLIMATE CHANGE

Unless climate change is halted or reversed, the area of the globe suitable for coffee cultivation may shrink 50 percent by the year 2050, a recent report indicates. "Ultimately, climate change is likely to push many producers out of coffee altogether," writes Corey Watts, a researcher at the Climate Institute of Australia.[53] Certainly small farmers, with their less robust resources, will suffer disproportionately. Although some farmers will be able to move higher in altitude, the soil becomes thinner and poorer as one goes up. Everything from wind and rain to the spread of broca varies in unfortunate ways or increases in damage inflicted as the globe warms. If a few farmers in California benefit, many others in countries that depend on coffee exports for a large part of national income will lose. A rise in average temperatures of 2°C in Uganda, for example, would reduce the area suitable for robusta to a small fraction of what it is today.[54] We have seen the way that climate change aggravated the problem of rust in Central America.

What might be done to save coffee? The obvious but probably least realistic answer is to significantly reduce global carbon emissions and greenhouse gases.

Planting more shade trees, sequestering carbon in certain plants, and applying more mulch can help—but they avail little in the face of relentless warming.

Be prepared to have your children pay more for coffee than you do, and for the possibility that your grandchildren may have a hard time finding it. When they do, it may well be robusta.

Two approaches to growing coffee, barring unexpected, vast changes in supply and demand, seem to be possibilities in keeping farmers afloat. One is to raise low-grade coffee without extensive inputs, as happens with robusta in Vietnam. The other is to grow high-quality coffee for which buyers are willing to spend good, or outrageous, money. It is the people in the middle, the majority, who suffer during years of oversupply. As consumers in the developed world and in producing countries like Brazil, China, Kenya, and Colombia drink more and better coffee, it will be possible for more farmers to make decent money. But many smaller farms, if they survive at all, must turn largely to other crops.

The best path toward greater social justice in the coffee industry is to get more people to drink more and better coffee. Chapter 3 examines patterns of coffee consumption around the world, as well as what needs to happen to make green beans into coffee liquor.

3

Roasting Coffee,
Making Coffee Drinks

Coffee is now better than beer or sex.

—Professor William Ristenpart, chemical engineer at UCD[1]

The most popular undergraduate elective course at the University of California, Davis (UCD) is "The Design of Coffee: An Engineering Approach." In 2016, it enrolled about fifteen hundred students, more than Human Sexuality or Introduction to Brewing and Beer. That's why Professor Ristenpart bragged about coffee's status.

In the class, students get their hands dirty while they learn how to roast, grind, and make coffee drinks, at least at an entry level. They engage in reverse engineering by taking the bottom off a Mr. Coffee® machine and trying to figure out how it works. They do all of that, and fulfill a science requirement, without using any more math than addition and subtraction. A course with good coffee but without math—how great is that?

It's even possible to major in coffee at the school. The rise of coffee classes at UCD is a hopeful sign for the specialty coffee industry. Certainly only a handful of all the students taking The Design of Coffee will enter the business. Yet many of the participants will talk about their experiences and promote their newly refined tastes to other people. This is really what specialty coffee needs: consumer education, or, even better, sophistication. That's a serious word that will be explored below.

So what kind of coffee is "better"—that is, most popular around the world? Maybe "it's true: Americans [and others] like to drink bad coffee."[2] Well, they don't know or don't think it's all that bad, but they do know that the grocery store coffee in a plastic tub is cheap and that instant is easy to make. For those who care more about the quality of coffee and are willing to pay a little extra for something delicious, the picture of who drinks what can be somewhat disheartening. Yet bright spots can be found in many places, at UCD and other campuses, in burgeoning consumption in a number of major countries, and in increased awareness of quality among younger Americans.

You can do a simple taste test at home, and any coffee drinker will be able to sense significant differences. Invite at least two unsuspecting people to try coffee in a blind test. Find a capsule or pod machine. Your friends have them, or maybe you have opted for convenience. There is no shame in that, but do consider other options. For now, get a jar of instant coffee; I recommend the smallest one available. Next go to the best local coffee shop near you. Buy a cup to go, preferably of light roast, and take it as quickly as you can to your test site. It doesn't matter if it cools off some. Make a cup of the instant as per the instructions, and make another cup with the capsule machine. Now get your guests to sip and slurp. Celebrate or mourn the results. You are on your way to becoming a coffee cupper (professional taster).

Coffee drinkers can be divided into the more or less sophisticated on one side and the lovers of convenience on the other. Most imbibers around the world prefer soluble (instant) or ground coffee from a grocery store. That's where the majority of robusta goes. Sales of instant coffee in 2013 amounted to some $31 billion globally and are growing steadily, already making up about one-third of the coffee market. Much instant is consumed in countries where coffee is not a long-standing tradition, namely Eastern Europe and China.[3] Of course, the same kind of ease in making a beverage applies to tea and helps explain its enduring popularity.

The hopeful part of convenience for the specialty industry is that people often start trying coffee with soluble. From instant, some of them move on to better cups. Russians, for example, are steadily switching to fresh brewed coffee. Ukrainians would if their economy was doing better. Young Chinese flock to Starbucks and other stores.

Pods are the intermediate step. As use of pods/capsules has swelled, their increased use has made Keurig Green Mountain the number one seller of coffee for home use in America, at $2.75 billion in 2014. Folgers rang in at $1.56 billion, Starbucks (packaged coffee) at $950 million, Maxwell House (Kraft Foods) at $820 million, and Dunkin' at $420 million.[4]

The J. M. Smucker Company, which owns the labels Folgers, Dunkin' Donuts packaged coffee, and Dunkin' K-cups, plus several lesser-known brands, brought in a profit of $645.9 million in the U.S. on sales of $2.239 billion worth of coffee in 2016.[5] Not bad for the gang from Ohio.

Starbucks' global profit ("consolidated operating income," referring to all expenses including taxes and accounting write-offs) was $4.2 billion in fiscal 2016, mostly from its more than 25,000 stores.[6] But much of that money came from sales of milk drinks like lattes, which put a lot of milk onto an espresso base. Consumption worldwide of espresso-based drinks rose three times from 2008 to 2015.[7] In general, the more milk and flavorings in a cup of "coffee," the higher the profit margin. Fiscal 2016 marked record sales and profits for Starbucks, with much of the growth coming from the Far East, especially China.

Calories rise more or less in tandem with the price of a drink: a Starbucks 16-ounce pumpkin spice latte has 380 calories, 120 of them from fat.[8] One of the leading contenders for the most calories in a coffee-based drink, if not the current champion, is Krispy Kreme's Mocha Dream Chiller, 20 ounces. It has 1,050 calories and 41 grams of total fat. That makes the drink, says *HuffPost*, equal to 6.17 White Castle cheeseburgers.[9] Putting such beverages into your body, except as a rare treat of something that resembles a milkshake, probably ruins any health benefits you might get from coffee alone, a subject covered in chapter 4.

The number two chain in the world, Costa Coffee, based in the UK and owned now by Whitbread, operated 3,401 stores in 2016. Like Starbucks, the company is aggressively expanding. Costa's global revenues in 2016 were £1.201 billion, or about $1.563 billion at the exchange rate of fall 2017. For the fiscal year 2015/16, Costa's profits were £153.5 million, or $199.76 million.[10] All stores in the two companies, as well as in McCafés, Peet's, and so on, aim to have each of their coffees taste the same, from London to Seattle to Beijing. Occasionally something like "special reserve" will appear in such outlets. But on a day-to-day basis, the coffee must be the same around the world. That imposes a limit on the subtlety and quality in the cup; not enough excellent coffee is grown to supply the voracious thirst of the big chain customers. Nor do the global outfits want to charge serious money for a fine cup of coffee, especially when they concentrate on milk drinks with a little espresso in them.

Several smaller chains and roasteries that have provided good to excellent coffee for years have recently been purchased by JAB Holdings, owned by a wealthy and fiercely independent German family. Since 2012, JAB has spent more than $40 billion to sweep up Peet's, Keurig Green Mountain, Caribou, and Jacobs Douwe Egberts, companies that did not sell expensive, especially high-quality coffee. The German clan also now has its eye on Dunkin' stores, which would give it 3,200 additional outlets in 36 countries. As of this writing, the deal has not gone through. Beyond those purchases, JAB has acquired two highly regarded medium-size roasters and coffee shop chains, Stumptown and Intelligentsia. Even more recently, Nestlé has acquired controlling interest in Blue Bottle Coffee. Incidentally, if you want casual food to go with your coffee, you can choose from other newly purchased JAB lines, among them Einstein Bagels, Krispy Kreme doughnuts, and Panera sandwiches. Consolidation, a 150-year-old story in the coffee business, marches on.

So far, the acquisition of Stumptown and Intelligentsia does not seem to have affected their offerings of quality coffee. To the further relief of many in specialty coffee, JAB has not gobbled up smaller roasters. Thus whatever the ultimate fate of Intelligentsia, Stumptown, and Blue Bottle may be, excellent coffee will probably still be available from them as well as others—that is, as long as global climate permits.

JAB will surely devote attention to quality, but the same limits that affect Starbucks and its peers apply to the German family's lesser brands. Another indication of the way that low- to middle-quality coffee dominates the market is the form in which coffee for home use is sold. Whole bean sales in the U.S. have languished under $1 billion annually since 2000, while ground coffee sales rose from about $4 billion per year to $12 billion in 2014.[11] Any serious roaster or barista will say that it's far better to buy whole beans and grind them just before making a cup to drink.

Capsules and pods, the second most convenient way of making cups of coffee after soluble, have also seen their sales shoot up. These "single serving" containers were just getting started in 2000. The research company Packaged Facts reported that recently the market for pod coffee in the U.S. has been growing at 18 percent or more per year and forecast that total sales of "single-cup" portions would reach $4.37 billion in 2015.[12] Data on that point are not yet available, but the figure seems likely. However, some observers of this sector feel that the single-serve market has become saturated and that future rapid growth is unlikely.

Still, the rest of the world will probably see increased use of capsules. A report released in September 2016 found that global sales of pod and capsule coffee would soon overtake "standard roast and ground coffee." Purchases of pods rose 29.5 percent over the previous twelve months, in nearly a billion households surveyed in thirty-five countries.

JAB's Keurig capsules are battling Nestlé's Nespresso, pitting a German company against a Swiss one. To date, Keurig dominates in the U.S., Nespresso in Europe. Some of the responsibility or blame for Nestlé pods' growth must attach to the "Clooney effect," as ads across Europe feature George Clooney, "the face of Nespresso," about to sip a pod drink.

Sophistication on display. The Clooney effect on a fashionable Berlin street, 2017.
Photo by Robert Thurston

The rise of foodstore pod/capsule sales brought the worldwide total value for the twelve months prior to September 2016 to £137.5 million (about $177.28 million).[13] Most of this growth occurred in Europe, as the continent's economy expanded slightly.

It is possible to buy reusable pods or capsules compatible with many machines and fill them with specialty coffee bought from a quality roastery. But that is too much trouble for many people, which is a double shame, as ordinary capsules end up in landfills. K cups made recently are partly recyclable, but first the top must be cut off and the used coffee grounds and paper cleaned out. Billions of the early versions cannot be recycled at all. This mess led John Sylvan, the inventor of K cups, to say that, "I feel bad sometimes that I ever did it."[14]

Beyond the environmental and quality issues with capsule coffee, it is far more expensive per cup than using ground coffee in a filter cone, French press, or any home machine. Oliver Strand of the *New York Times* calculated the cost of Nespresso and K Cup coffee at $50–$51 a pound.[15] That's getting into the range of Kona's best coffees, and is several times the cost of excellent coffees from other regions rated at well above 90 points. Since some 74 percent of all coffee is consumed at home in the U.S., the various costs of pods and capsules mount up fast.[16]

Outside the home, Starbucks dominates coffee's cultural landscape, as demonstrated in songs and innumerable cartoons. As the company's reach exploded in the 1990s and early 2000s, the *New Yorker* could hardly feature enough satire about the phenomenon. One drawing depicts a man and a woman sitting in a shop; he says to her, "Are we in this Starbucks or the one down the street?"[17] A great jab at the Mermaid is the line, superimposed on a cup of her coffee, "Instead of going to Starbucks, I make my coffee at home, yell my name out incorrectly, then light a $5 bill on fire."[18] (My only problem with this approach is burning the five!) In 1998, *The Onion* published an article titled, "New Starbucks Opens in Rest Room of Existing Starbucks."[19] The country music song "There's a Starbucks Where the Starbucks Used to Be," by John Wesley Harding (2011), sums up the way the Mermaid has entered our consciousness and culture.

Yet specialty coffee, of which Starbucks is a part, must be grateful to former CEO Howard Schultz and his ultra-energetic drive to put his firm's stores everywhere. In 1991 there were some 1,650 independent shops in the U.S. By 2015, the total had risen to 31,490.[20] Of all the stores open in the U.S. in 2016,

Starbucks ran 13,172.[21] Peet's was a distant second at 236 stores, although other outlets also sell the company's coffee. Starbucks made Americans aware that coffee could taste pretty good. That realization in turn encouraged customers to look to local, possibly better coffee.

The same effect occurred in Europe. In Germany, for instance, it used to be common to find more or less decent *Kaffee und Kuchen* (coffee and a piece of cake or pastry) at many restaurants or cafés—but hardly on every corner in every town. Then on another visit in 2010, I walked the length of the world's longest pedestrian-only street, Heidelberg's *Hauptstrasse* (main street). In the first four blocks from one end point at the old Fish Market, I counted twenty places that served coffee, including a Starbucks and a Costa store. Alas, a more recent experience in Berlin convinced me that the German expression *Maschinenkaffee* still describes most of what you get in that city.

With all the new coffee shops around the globe and the burgeoning interest in specialty coffee, the level of training from farmer to barista has risen impressively in many places. On the other hand, deskilling is also widespread in specialty coffee, as baristas operate "super automatic" espresso machines that need only the push of a button. These devices grind the coffee, tamp it into a portafilter (where the coffee is now called a puck, since it is now about the size of a hockey puck), and force water through it. The barista has only to show off the tattoos and serve.

The ease of the automatic process can be compared to other machines on which the grind must be adjusted every so often by hand, as temperature, humidity, and even air pressure can change the way a shot tastes. On the most sophisticated but still manually operated espresso machines, the barista can change the pressure of the water while pulling the shot to bring out maximum flavor. Different single-origin coffees will, of course, deliver shots with quite different flavor profiles, even to the extent of producing layered tastes. Developing a flavorful and complex espresso blend is almost a world unto itself.

Plenty of hard work and development of skills are essential in other aspects of bringing out flavor. With a generous amount of time, money, and practice, many people have the raw sensory talent to become a certified Q grader (cupper), a title given by the Coffee Quality Institute (CQI). Armed with the Q title, you are qualified to identify defects in green coffee, rate coffee on the 100-point scale, and render judgments on the qualities or lack thereof in any brewed coffee.

This pre–World War I Italian espresso machine worked by gravity. Hot water was fed to the top chamber on each side and then allowed to pass down through ground coffee. The term "espresso" at first meant only quick service; the word was intended to be linked to express trains in Italy, and coffee made from early machines of this type was first sold at railway stations. Only with the invention of a machine by Gaggia in 1947 that forced water through the ground coffee did modern espresso arrive. At first the Italians called it "cream coffee" in both their language and in English, a reference to the light brown layer on top of the drink. We have now swung back to the Italian word for cream to call that layer crema.

From the collection of Enrico Maltoni; photo by Robert Thurston

However, there are limits to anyone's sniffing/tasting ability. Avery Gilbert, a long-time sniffer in the perfume industry, says the idea that aroma experts can detect 10,000 or 30,000 smells is nonsense. No scientific studies support that kind of claim. "Wine snobs" do not appeal to Gilbert. He does like the flavor wheels adopted by several industries, beginning with a "practical smell classification for beer" created in the 1970s by the Danish chemist Morten Meilgaard. His work helped lead to the "Wine Aroma Wheel" produced by Professor Ann Noble and colleagues at UC Davis in 1984. Now there are two versions of coffee flavor wheels. All of these graphic depictions of aromas and tastes—for maple products, cheese, brandy, natural perfume, sewage, and "unifloral honey," among others—are pie charts divided into categories. Does your beer taste earthy, like potatoes or grass, or even "skunky"? If the latter, the brew has been oxidized.[22] Coffee can be "sweaty," "hidey," medicinal, or—much better—floral, fruity, chocolaty, or malty.

Gilbert notes studies that show people untrained in sniffing have trouble identifying even a single ingredient in a mix of scents. When psychologist David Laing added a "target odor" and asked subjects if they could detect it in a mixture, few people could find it in a blend of more than three odors. Professionals were better at this task, but "they failed to pick more than three odors from the mix." No one "could bust the four-odor limit."[23] Since we know that our sense of taste is overwhelmingly determined by scent, as flavors touch the tongue but more importantly make contact with the olfactory nerves in the roof of the mouth, the four-odor limit should apply to the taste of coffee as well. Wine tasters often have this kind of problem or worse; the numerous articles describing the inability of wine "experts" to distinguish between expensive and cheap wines, or even to recognize a white wine when it has merely been dyed red, undermine faith in fancy descriptions of wine flavors.[24]

When strings of adjectives are applied to any consumer product, from perfume to coffee, the verbiage can become overly fussy and unhelpful, except perhaps to professional tasters. They can try to lock in the taste of a particular cup of coffee by freighting it with loads of descriptors. But to my perhaps simple mind the idea that a single coffee can have flavors ranging through "caramel-coated raisin and all-spice . . . chocolate roast tones, burned sugar . . . honey and caramel . . . high percent cacao bar . . . darker fruit notes, plum and concord grape" and even more is way over the top.[25]

Here is an old-style Italian espresso machine, made in 1981, stripped to show the boiler with a relief valve in the center; the levers—which are pulled down to make coffee (hence the expression "to pull a shot"); the tubes that deliver water or steam to the front of the machine; and the portafilters, one "hooked in" to the left group head, the other resting on a bench beneath the machine. Not visible are heavy springs below the lever mechanisms. Pressure during the shot can be varied by holding a lever at different positions. This machine is capable of running on electricity or gas. Lever machines have recently made a comeback, although most espresso makers capable of varying pressure during the shot have a simple handle at the top of the group head that moves horizontally and requires little strength to manage.
Photo by Robert Thurston

Still worse is a claim from the company Ninety Plus Coffee about its green coffee sold, as mentioned in chapter 2, in September 2017 for $2,273 a pound. A company spokesman, 2014 World Brewers Cup Champion Stefanos Domatiotis, described the coffee's liquor as "having notes of white peach, narcissus, grapefruit zest, lilac, loquat, raspberry, jackfruit, lyric, buoyant, cacao nib, star anise, guava, cola, wisteria, dried orange, maple syrup, plush, velvety, and, last but not least, 'the color pink.'" To make matters still murkier, Ninety Plus added that the coffee evokes sensations of "multifaceted inspiration, erotic innervation, epiphany, possibility," and "femininity."[26]

This is flatulent nonsense. Besides the impossibility of a human being, or any creature, having the ability to taste all those flavors in one cup, obviously no one can taste the color pink. As for sensations of femininity, I have no comment. The description is reminiscent of the attempts by perfumers and men's cologne makers to persuade customers that their products evoke emotions and raise sex appeal to fabulous heights.

In my own store, I have seen customers' eyes glaze over when I have talked too much about flavor notes in coffee. In specialty coffee, a fine line exists between encouraging sophistication and driving people away.

The specialty world has a new set of serious descriptors and degrees of intensity for them, developed by World Coffee Research with input from some of the best-known people in the business. Called Sensory Lexicon 2.0, this tool for the industry and other fanatics "doesn't have categories for 'good' and 'bad' attributes, nor does it allow for ranking coffee quality. It is purely a descriptive tool, which allows you to say with a high degree of confidence that a coffee tastes or smells like X, Y, or Z." The intensity of any taste or characteristic, from lemon through pepper to animalic and way beyond, can be noted on a scale of 1 to 15. Grading intensity "allows us to compare differences among coffees with a significantly higher degree of precision" than other methods have permitted. The lexicon makers believe that, when cuppers are properly trained, their system will enable professionals to speak the same way about coffee anywhere in the world.[27] However, WCR warns that the system is not a substitute for cupping and scoring, but rather a supplemental means of talking precisely about any coffee's characteristics.

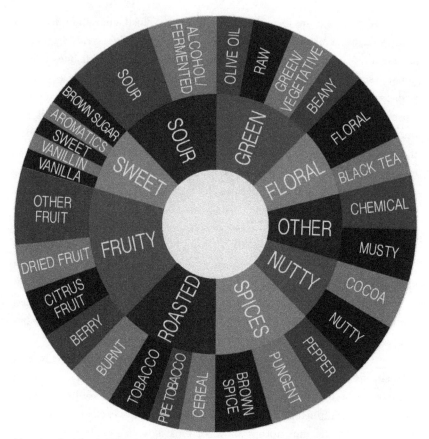

Here is a highly simplified version of the "coffee taster's flavor wheel," of which there are now several types. Other versions are easily found on the internet. This illustration provides the basic categories for flavor notes in coffee. Please use your imagination to think about what more subtle distinctions might lie beyond "berry" and so forth.
Illustration by Lara Thurston

Another, much less developed vocabulary dominates the specialty coffee industry today for coffee service. *Barista* came from fascist Italy. Like so much connected with coffee, the word has its own narrative: Mussolini's regime wanted a new word for people who served coffee. Everything had to be modern in 1930s Italy, including words. *Barman* and *bartender* were too English/ American, so the dictator's wordsmiths concocted a new term that would still remind people to come up to the bar for a coffee. Or at least the timing is right: The *Oxford English Dictionary* dates the Italian word from 1939–1940, and the first use of *barista* in English is from 1982, in a book by the Austrian Paul Hofmann, *Rome: The Sweet Tempestuous Life*. In that same year, Howard Schultz joined an existing company, Starbucks, as director of retail operations and marketing. He claimed that his inspiration for a new kind of coffee shop struck on a visit to Milan.

The migration of *barista* is only the latest phase of coffee's global movement, from old French *barre* through English *bar* to the Italian word to America and the rest of the world. The term's travels show not only the influence of Italian on the world of coffee, from a country which still makes some of the best espresso machines and grinders, but also the way coffee itself and coffee culture have spread across the earth. In Russia, China, India, Brazil, and on and on, *cappuccino* is pronounced somewhat differently. But saying the word in anything close to the Italian way will get you a cup in chain and local stores.

Coffee, or rather specialty coffee, has been in its "third wave" for decades. Much debate revolves around the chronology and meaning of the first and second waves. These designations have to do with the ways in which coffee has been sold and/or handled. In my opinion, the first wave referred to the days before coffee was branded—that is, people would go into a general store and buy coffee, not distinguished or named in any other way, from a barrel. Sometimes the barrel would be next to another containing smelly food, particularly fish. Usually the buyer got green coffee to roast at home. The second wave, my thinking continues, began after the American Civil War; it was then that brand names and packaging, for example, Hills Brothers, appeared and dominated the growing market. Railroads and steamship lines tied the American and other markets together, making it possible to find the same food products in Boston and Seattle, Bremen and Munich. The third inundation opened in the 1960s and '70s as more and more roasters and coffeehouses began to take considerable care with the beans. Now there is even a claim that coffee has entered a fourth wave, riding on the best current methods of making drinks.[28] But I do not see any essential difference between the notion of a fourth wave and the idea of the third wave. Why not just be happy that many people make every effort to produce great coffee?

Whatever the present phase is numbered, it relates only to specialty coffee. Commodity or commercial coffee has hardly changed since branding and packing of roasted beans first began. Beans in that category are not carefully selected and handled and usually cannot be traced back to a country of origin. The goal of Folgers, for example, is to make the coffee taste the same no matter the time of year or the origin of the beans. "Fungibility" is the term used; that is, Folgers and other similar brands must find beans that can be substituted for other beans not seasonally available, and still come up with the old familiar taste.

Consumers want such coffee to be strong. The result is a hit-and-run beverage: the taste and impact in the mouth are powerful but will disappear quickly. There is no subtlety, no lingering flavor, except for a hint of burnt metal. Antidotes are available in the form of cream or sugar. Somewhat crudely put, any coffee that comes in a jar or plastic tub in a grocery store is commodity stuff; anything that comes in a bag is specialty. Thus Starbucks and Peet's are specialty, although some say that packaged Starbucks in food stores is not. Folgers is definitely not, and does not care to be.

Fine; many people are not interested in sophisticated food and drink. Part of that outlook results from the snobbishness that frequently oozes forth from specialty food purveyors, from the business of cheese to wine to exotic olive oil and vinegar. Commodity coffee is served in, say, a pancake house by a person dressed simply, without the effects that baristas have often adopted: tattoos all over bare arms and up the neck, silly hats, pieces of metal stuck in the face, and wooden spools in the earlobes. This is not what middle America, even in Portland, wants to see when being served coffee.

COFFEE CONSUMPTION AROUND THE WORLD

The USDA says that "global consumption is forecast [for 2018] at a record 158 million bags," which is very good news. "World ending stocks" in 2016/17 have declined to 34 million bags from a high of about 43 million in 2014/15.[29] Such figures have engendered optimism within the coffee industry, although the ending stocks—that is, unsold coffee—remain substantial.

But in the U.S., despite all the new shops and interest, coffee consumption is not rising much. Imports into the country in 1990 amounted to 21,007,000 bags; the 2015 figure, for a much larger population, was 27,708,000. By contrast, the European Union in 1990 imported 45,781,000 bags and in 2015

76,896,000 bags. Domestic consumption, bearing in mind that 15–20 percent by weight will be lost during roasting, has also risen nicely in several producing countries: Brazilians in 2000/01 drank up 13,200,000 bags and in 2016/17 downed drinks made from 20,500,000 bags. Vietnam's domestic intake rose in the same period from 402,000 bags to 2,300,000. Figures for several countries show impressive gains: Vietnam's total rose by 178 percent and Russia's by 397 percent from 2015/16 to the following year.[30]

Increases in consumption in producing countries represent a particularly promising development for the coffee industry, as more coffee drunk on the spot means more shops with jobs that boost more people onto at least the bottom rungs of the middle class. Moreover, every café I have visited, from Kenya to Honduras—supposedly the murder capital of the world—to Chicago has been a safe space where people are not, with rare exceptions, exposed to violence.

Who drinks coffee? First, who drinks the most coffee in the world? Some articles proclaim the Netherlands the champion, one claiming 2.4 cups downed per person each day.[31] But that is wrong. First, what does "cup" mean? A standard American measured cup is 8 ounces. However, a small cup of coffee here is often more like 6 ounces. A cup doesn't mean much of anything elsewhere. Of course, most countries use the metric system, and in lands like Italy and Britain, espresso-based drinks are far more popular than drip (brewed) coffee. Forget cups; the question needs to be approached in another way: how many kilos of coffee are consumed in a given country? The International Coffee Association provides the figures.[32] From them, it's easy to calculate:

Finland is the champ by a long shot. The country has about 5.5 million inhabitants, who consumed 1.1 million bags of coffee (remember, 60 kilograms each) in 2015, or some 145.2 million pounds. That works out to be 12.2 kilos (26.84 pounds) per man, woman, transgenders, and children per year. Those numbers do not allow for weight loss during roasting. But that loss is pretty much the same anywhere. Meanwhile, Finland re-exports only 7.1 percent of the coffee it imports.

The Netherlands can't possibly be the winner, because the Dutch, with a population of almost 17 million, imported not much more than the Finns in 2015, 1.5 million total bags. That raw figure puts consumption per capita at 5.3 kilos a year, or 11.66 pounds. Even this number is misleading, as the Dutch, long-time coffee roasters, re-exported 28.1% of the coffee they brought into the country.

Going further and doing the math, ICO figures put Swedish consumption at 10.1 kilos per person annually and Norwegian at 8.68. Even Germany outpaces the Netherlands, at 6.5 kilos. Sorry, Dutch people. I still love your country anyway.

The U.S. is far behind. America does import more bags of coffee than anyone else, and coffee grows in Hawaii, California, and Puerto Rico. But we don't actually drink all that much. 23.8 million bags entered the country in 2015, but per capita consumption was 4.5 kilos per year (9.9 pounds). America also re-exports coffee, some 16 percent of imports.

Further down the list, the UK is at 3.3 kilos, Russia at 1.69, and China at a lowly .83 kilos. But as Russia's economy slowly regains strength, and China's youth focus more on coffee as a hip drink, consumption in both countries will rise.

So there we have it. Go north to find the hard-core coffee drinkers.

WHAT IS "SOPHISTICATION"?

Before delving further into who consumes coffee, a brief excursion into the meaning of "sophistication" is in order. Like any reasonable study of words and what they convey written over the past forty years, this book draws on the work of a French thinker, or rather from the clearer parts of his work. The sociologist Pierre Bourdieu rose to academic stardom by doing more than anyone else to explore "taste," in the sense of good versus bad, "sophisticated" versus naïve. He argued that taste was a way of "legitimating social differences," that is, of separating the coarse, vulgar, or ordinary folk from those who value more sublime and refined experiences. How does anyone acquire good taste? That process is largely a matter of accumulating cultural or educational "capital," by which Bourdieu meant exposure to ideas of what is elevated. Educational capital can be roughly ascertained by looking at anyone's level of formal education.

Snobby, yes; related to concepts of taste and to money, absolutely. The specialty coffee industry aims to follow the trajectory of the wine industry, especially in the U.S. If we take a starting point for wine sales in 1962—at the peak of per capita coffee consumption in America, incidentally—wine consumption per person was .9 gallons, or 3.4 liters.[33] By 2016, wine intake here had risen more than three times per capita, to 2.9 gallons. Retail wine sales grew from $26.3 billion in 2000 to more than $60 billion in 2016. By contrast, the U.S. retail coffee market

A cupping class for young Hondurans, La Fe, Honduras. Here the students learn how to properly score coffee, to detect scents, and to keep careful records.
Photo by Robert Thurston

amounted to an estimated $48 billion in 2015, with specialty coffee making up about 55 percent of the total.[34] Good coffee lags far behind wine of any quality.

Forty to fifty years ago, wine was served in America only by people with direct connections or experience in Europe and by Jews on holy days. For most people here, wine seemed expensive, literally foreign to our taste, and snobbish. What changed those attitudes was not only the spread of vineyards but also a brilliant campaign by wine producers and enthusiasts to make the drink's appeal at once broader and more exotic. All those descriptors that almost no one can taste in wine suddenly seemed to spell out sophistication. The 100-point rating system for wine, developed in the 1970s by Robert M. Parker Jr., quickly became a way of marketing fermented grape juice. Looking at the number that some expert assigned to a given wine became an easy code for measuring taste and inflating the buyer's sense of sophistication.

Specialty coffee has borrowed the 100-point idea directly from the wine industry, as well as many of the adjectives applied to the taste of coffee. Even an essential kit of scents for training cuppers, *Le Nez du Café* (The Nose of Coffee), was modeled directly, and by the same creator, Jean Lenoir, on his *Le Nez du Vin* (The Nose of Wine). It will be no surprise that training one's sense of taste for wine or coffee begins with the nose.

What does sophistication mean in practice? Well, do you prefer "The Blue Danube" or a Mozart symphony? Careful; you may classify yourself. Of course, people may prefer Elvis one day and Beethoven the next, or their preference may change from hour to hour. Pierre Bourdieu was speaking in overall terms. In several surveys, he found that manual workers, domestic servants, and shop-keepers liked the "Blue Danube" a lot; teachers in higher education did not. Workers disliked Bach's "The Well-Tempered Clavier," but people employed in higher education and "art producers" enjoyed it. Bourdieu found that the higher the level of education people have, the more they disdain pictures of "objects of popular admiration," among them sunsets.[35]

Becoming sophisticated, although Bourdieu did not use the word much, is a matter of learning a cultural code. I would add that it takes time and some dedication to the idea of elevating oneself to learn any such code. We are not genetically programmed to enjoy abstract art, for instance; we must be taught that it is worthwhile. Generally, Bourdieu wrote, professionals—art critics and so on—teach others about taste. And the upper classes set the pace, because they have the time, money, and inherited things and ideas that allow them to make contrasts with new ideas. Anything novel needs to be compared and evaluated against old objects and ideas, which are not all to be discarded lightly. Some are kept as earlier markers of quality. In Europe, the aristocracy had traditional ways (which it defined) pretty well in hand by the Middle Ages. The upper crust lived among old objects. Those factors gave the elite more credibility as arbiters of the new. Aristocrats invented taste and stressed that having taste separated them from the common herd. Then, in one of the ways new or "good" taste spreads, it filters down to the classes lower on the social scale. Publicity certainly helps; specialized wine magazines make the case for wines. Put such a periodical out on your coffee table, and people will see that you are sophisticated.

Bourdieu also noted that the upper classes disdain "plentiful and good" meals in favor of the "original and exotic."[36] Exotic in this sense meant at first from another country or part of the world. That is why many specialty German food stores used to bear the sign *Kolonialwaren*, "colonial goods." By the eighteenth century, well-off Germans had developed a taste for *Genussmittel*, which might be translated as "articles of pleasure." Wolfgang Schivelbusch has referred to them as "tastes of paradise."[37] And where was paradise, if it could be said to exist on earth—which was a common belief or pious wish among medieval and later thinkers. Paradise was certainly not in bloody, dirty Germany or England. It had to be far away, unknown or nearly so, mystical, and, in a word, exotic. Products from there had to taste different and quite good, or at least new; if they induced unfamiliar but pleasant sensations to Europeans, so much the better. David Jacobson, who translated Schivelbusch's book *Tastes of Paradise: A Social History of Spices, Stimulants, and Intoxicants*, added a comment about the word *Genussmittel*. It "denotes," he wrote, "a group of substances for human consumption which are eaten, drunk, or inhaled to create pleasures of the senses, as opposed to those foods and beverages consumed as necessities. . . . [The word] therefore also implies that these substances are luxuries for sybaritic enjoyment, means for creating epicurean delights and, by extension, a state of sensual bliss."[38]

This all borders on "erotic innervation," and Jacobson is overstating the case for substances like pepper. Yet we must consider the general blandness of European food before spices arrived from far away. In the late Middle Ages, they came especially from India or the archipelago originally called the Spice Islands (the East Indies, Java, Borneo, and many others), so dubbed by the piratical whites who first sailed to them. But there is no question that spices from the Far (an exotic term) East struck Europeans as having spiritual qualities of one sort or another. "Spicy" quickly came to mean exciting, racy, stimulating. Joseph Addison (1672–1719) wrote in the early English periodical *Spectator*, which was based in Button's Coffeehouse, of the "pleasures of the imagination." For him, "Whatever is *new* or *uncommon* . . . serves us for a kind of refreshment, and takes off from that satiety we are apt to complain of in our usual and ordinary entertainments."[39] While every new development, for example, AIDS, may not be refreshing, Addison clearly endorsed the appeal of the exotic.

The Spice Islands were east of what, precisely? Terms like "the West" are fairly recent, dating only to the eighteenth century and then only in a limited way. Going back two hundred to three hundred years earlier, the literary scholar Timothy Morton shows, seafaring European nations, from Portugal to England, thought of the East Indies as "the earthly paradise, east of Eden." The trade winds blew marvelous scents in the direction of Europe; writers made the image of eastern trees "breathing spice" a regular motif in the eighteenth-century En-lightenment.[40] A vivid imagination is also important in the development of taste.

Specialty coffee has often been called "the affordable luxury." The concept of luxury implies not only the means to purchase exotic items, however small they may be, but also the time and the cultural knowledge needed to enjoy them. Morton, and to some extent Schivelbusch, maintain that the quest for spices and the ability to appreciate them marked the beginning of consumer society, even of capitalism itself. The "humanist distaste for luxurious consumption" had to be left behind.[41] This is not the place to discuss that issue in depth; suffice it to say that those mostly grim old thinkers of the sixteenth and seventeenth centuries, from Erasmus to Locke, were conservative about consumption. An outlook that encouraged thrift and modesty did not encourage trying new tastes.

Schivelbusch notes that spices became new markers of status in the late Middle Ages, while the flavors were still rare in Europe. "Social connections, balance of power, wealth, prestige, and all manner of fantasies were 'tasted': what would become matters of social and cultural 'taste' or fashion, were first matters of physical tasting."[42] This too may be somewhat exaggerated; Euro-pean nobles had long demonstrated their status by dressing in fabrics, for ex-ample, that were unavailable or even illegal for common folk, before spices ap-peared regularly upon dining tables. In the medieval period, aristocrats touted their nobility, in lineage and manners, in contrast to the English peasants or *villeins*—same root as *vile*—or to the French *paysans*, those who worked on the land (*pays*) in the dirt and who were themselves dirty. Yet something of the argument about exotic sources of identity and status can also be made for silk: it first came from the fabled East.

The story of images of the East as they appeared in Western Europe is complex. After a Christian army soundly defeated the Turks at Vienna in 1683, portrayals of Turks and Arabs often became critical and dismissive, as in the phrase "bugger the Turk." Buffoonish café signs like a turbaned Turk's head with a huge nose became popular around the same time. Yet the flip side of this disdain was that "the East" continued to retain its mystical, romantic allure. The first translation into English of *One Thousand and One [Arabian] Nights* appeared in 1706, and new translations were published regularly into the 1880s.

Despite the negative images of "eastern" peoples, the connections of exoti-cism to the role of coffee in introducing new tastes to Western Europe should

Coffee drinking spread through the French upper classes by the eighteenth century. The original painting is titled Le petit dejeuner *(Breakfast), c. 1770–1820, but probably closer to 1770, given the styles. The artist is unknown.*
Library of Congress, Prints and Photographs Division

already be evident. *Coffea arabica* can suggest fantasies of the harem and of the lush gardens and strange animals that Europeans encountered as they ventured far from home. The historian Brian Cowan has made the tie between the exotic and coffee explicit in his discussion of seventeenth-century English "virtuosi," well-to-do connoisseurs of the unusual "who sought to associate themselves with an international world of elite cultural interests. . . . Coffee was one of the curiosities that captured the fancy of England's virtuoso community."[43]

Even though these early English seekers after knowledge did not specifically look for new tastes, they were deeply interested in the search for new truths and for the economic and scientific value of things they encountered. In the case of coffee, as with various other novelties for English travelers, the new product needed help from experts, if only self-styled, to become a regular part of life back home. "Many virtuosi publicized and promoted the widespread use of the new commodity, even when its medical virtues were called into question. . . . Without the culture of virtuosity to nurture it in its infancy, coffee drinking may have remained little more than an odd Turkish habit with only a few English practitioners."[44]

HOW COFFEE SPREAD AROUND THE GLOBE

That is how coffee came to England. In other lands, the drink also produced new sensations, almost invariably pleasurable. Here are lines from a poem written at the beginning of the 1800s by the French abbot Jacques Delille:

I had hardly tasted your fragrant liquor
Suddenly, from your climate heat penetrated
Agitating all my senses, without cares, without jolts
My thoughts, more numerous, came in great waves
My spirit had been sad, arid, barren
[Now it] laughs, it is richly adorned.[45]

Tastes of Paradise indeed.

Ask any serious practitioner in specialty coffee about his or her first experience with a really good cup of coffee; you probably won't get a poem in response, but it's common to see a dreamy look come over the other person, who very probably remembers that cup well. I certainly do. So when good coffee grabs you, its hold is tight.

Where did coffee come from originally? Legends abound about how coffee beans came first to be eaten, then made into a drink. Maybe once upon a time there was a real person, Kaldi the goatherd, guarding a flock in Ethiopia, who noticed that his charges were extra frisky one day. He followed them and found that they were eating coffee cherries. More probably, that's just a cute story. Did Ethiopian warriors chew on coffee beans so they could march and fight longer while staying more alert? Such images are impossible to pin down.

Nor does anyone know where the word *coffee* came from. *Kahveh* or *qahwa* is an Arabic word for wine; maybe someone got a little confused about the beverage. Chapter 4 looks at the origin of words for coffee more deeply. *Kahveh* became the Turkish word for coffee. English took its word from the Dutch *kaffie* in 1582—that much we can be precise about. Café, caffè, Kaffee, kofe (Russian) and so on come from the same general linguistic vicinity.

The oldest known written reference to coffee dates from 1497, in a letter from a merchant of Tûr, at the southern tip of the Sinai Peninsula.[46] Coffee "came into general use in the lands of Islam sometime in the mid-fifteenth century." But there is "virtual silence" about when and how "the beverage insinuated itself into the society."[47] Sufi monks in what is today Yemen were drinking a coffee beverage by the late fifteenth century, apparently to help them stay awake and recite more prayers. The Sufis and others spread knowledge of the bean into Arabia, especially to Cairo, where Yemeni students at Al-Azhar University used it by the early 1500s. Coffee was already known in the Middle East before anyone wrote about it; at some point between 1470 and 1500, Arabs brought it from Yemen to Mecca and Medina. The "first authentic account of the origins of coffee" is found in an Arabic manuscript of 1587.[48] That simply means no one has found an earlier written tale of coffee's origins.

Probably coffee was not cultivated but merely picked from the ground or from the branches of wild trees, until the fifteenth century, when Yemenis started to build a remarkable system of terraces that climb steep hillsides. Many such terraces still exist. We do know that the first recorded coffeehouse anywhere was in operation in Damascus by 1534. Coffee got another boost when the Ottoman Turks occupied Yemen in 1536, which gave them a monopoly on the trade for a long time.

It was not long before knowledge of coffee reached the West. Leonhart Rauwolf, a physician and botanist from the German city of Augsburg, was a great exemplar of early modern Europeans who sought new tastes; he was a non-English virtuoso. He was the first Westerner to describe how coffee, which he encountered in Aleppo (now in Syria, and all but destroyed in recent fighting), was made and served. His *True Description of a Journey to the Morning Lands* (my abbreviated translation of his title) appeared in 1582. By "Morning Lands" he meant places east of Germany, lands where the sun came up—from his perspective. He called coffee "a very good drink" and was also impressed by "very fine gardens" in several places.[49]

Coffee crossed the Alps by 1596, and another legend has a Sufi monk from India, Baba Budan, smuggling coffee seeds tied in a cloth around his waist from Mecca to India in about 1600, or maybe 1685. Legends, after all, remain legends. In any case, coffee trees did reach southern India around that year. The Dutch acquired a viable tree in 1616—also much against the wishes of the Ottomans, who wanted to keep the trade to themselves. A major shipment of beans, still coming from Yemen, reached Venice in 1624. At that point, the drink was sold on the street by vendors who also served lemonade, and later chocolate drinks and tobacco for pipes. Coffee reached France, at Marseilles, in 1644, along with utensils to make and serve it. The Dutch were able to plant trees in Ceylon (Sri Lanka) in 1658 and in Java in 1699. All of this migration and trade was between seaports, of course.

Sultan Ahmet (Blue) Mosque, Istanbul, built 1609–1616. Every Western European traveler to Istanbul after 1616, and probably almost every traveler to the "East," would have seen this imposing mosque on a hill in the center of the city. It is an extremely impressive sight to this day.
Photographed by Miran Iranian between 1870 and 1900. Library of Congress

According to the French traveler Jean de Thévenot, who visited Istanbul in the mid-seventeenth century, "all sorts of people" frequented the city's coffee-houses. The customers were all male, and typically they might linger in a café and enjoy both the drink and the ever-present music.[50]

There is a debate about where the first Western coffeehouse appeared, in London or in Oxford. The evidence seems better for London's claim. At some point between 1652 and 1654, a public coffee service opened in London. William Ukers, a noted historian and promoter of coffee in the period 1910–1940, reproduced "the first coffee advertisement, 1652," from an original in the British Museum.[51] This early enterprise, located in London, was sponsored by two merchants of the Levant Company, chartered in 1605. One of the businessmen, Daniel Edwards, already enjoyed a reputation as a "prodigious drinker" of coffee, consuming "two or three Dishes" of it several times a day. Edwards had earlier met a young Greek in Smyrna (today Izmir, Turkey), Pascal Rosee (or Rosée), who now came to London to manage the new shop. Smyrna was already a lively center of international trade. The English were bringing home the sophistication that they found abroad and that Rauwolf and numerous others had described. Although Rosée's first place of business was apparently a shack whose shutters opened wide for service, it was not long before he and another associate set up a more stable shop.[52]

Coffee received a huge push in France in 1669 with the arrival of the Turkish ambassador Suleiman Aga at the court of Versailles. A large and imposing man who dressed in colorful robes, he soon became a hit with elegant French women, to whom he served coffee in porcelain cups and saucers. Porcelain was still not produced in Europe, partly owing to the lack up to that time of kaolin clay, found on the continent only in the eighteenth century. Aga epitomized the exotic at a European court that prided itself on creating or discovering the latest fashions and tastes.

A lively taste for porcelain can be neatly linked to the spread of coffee among the upper classes. Finally manufactured in Europe in 1708, and later at Meissen and Sèvres, for example, its lightness and translucence also helped produce a new experience in drinking hot beverages. Now the visual effect, enchanting for those who had never seen it before, added to the total impression made by coffee—and by tea as well. It's lucky that porcelain is too delicate to allow clinking cups, or we would be toasting each other with tea and coffee.

This cup, in the author's collection, is a modern reproduction of an Imperial Russian coffee cup and saucer first manufactured in the late eighteenth century by the Lomonosov Works in St. Petersburg.
Photo by Robert Thurston

Nothing is wrong with good old stoneware, sturdy and heavy as it is. But it does not let light through to play upon a beverage, and its long use in Europe made it an everyday object. When porcelain first arrived, and for a long time after, it was subtle and exotic, and its adoption helped both coffee and tea to become even more fashionable.

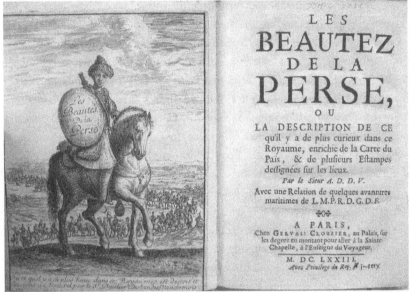

Frontispiece and title page of The Beauties of Persia, *written by André Daulier Deslandes and published in 1672. The book is typical of the times and its tastes for the Eastern exotic, especially what is "most curious." Daulier Deslandes has depicted himself as a Persian rider.*

Coffee service first proliferated in England and the rest of Britain. By the 1710s, London could claim 550 coffeehouses.[53] The Dutch, Germans, and French lagged behind the English, although not for long, in setting up coffeehouses. Dutch traders appear to have brought coffee to New Amsterdam (New York) and probably to Boston by the 1660s. Although one Dorothy Jones received a license to sell "coffee and cuchaletto" in Boston in 1670, the first record of an establishment in the city actually selling coffee to drink, the London Coffeehouse, dates to 1689. New York was a bit behind; the earliest record of a coffeehouse opening there is from 1696.[54] Coffee service first appeared on the continent in Hamburg, another cosmopolitan city, in 1677, and in Vienna by 1685—although coffee was known there earlier.[55] Paris welcomed its first serious location, the Café Procope, in 1689. Pretty much the farther east and inland one looks in Europe, the later coffee arrived; it is mentioned regularly in Russia only in the early nineteenth century.

As the French writer Felipe Ferré described the spread of the beverage on the continent, "Germany was touched somewhat later [than Britain or France] by this surging wave that was Coffeemania."[56] A striking indication of coffee's popularity in Germany, at least among the well-off, was Johann Sebastian Bach's *Coffee Cantata*, 1732. Bach took a break from writing religious music to simultaneously satirize and admire coffee. With words by Christian Friedrich Henrici, known as Picander, the cantata is called in German "Schweigt still, plaudert nicht"—Be quiet, don't chatter. The piece, first performed in Zimmermann's coffeehouse in Leipzig no later than 1735, describes a young woman's love, if not addiction, for coffee. Really a one-act comic operetta, the story features a father, Schlendrian, who is sick of hearing about the passion his daughter Liesgen feels for coffee. He threatens to deny her everything from ribbons to a husband if she won't give up the drink. She finally agrees, but lets all her suitors know that in fact they must provide her with coffee if they marry her; that must be stipulated in the marriage contract.

Although love of coffee is gently satirized, the cantata ends with a stanza about how "the cat does not leave the mouse," meaning that drinking coffee is a natural act. Mothers and grandmothers drank coffee, and "Who can blame the daughters?"[57]

In spreading coffee, the Dutch did the most at first. As noted, Dutch colonizers planted coffee in Java in 1696, only to see the trees destroyed by a flood. Undiscouraged, the Dutch planted again and were able to carry coffee beans from the islands in 1711.[58] But the French also did some heavy shipping. They brought coffee trees to their Caribbean colonies, notably Saint Domingue (Haiti), starting in 1715. From there the plant migrated south, reaching Brazil in 1727. The French also took coffee trees to the island of Bourbon (now Réunion) in the Indian Ocean off Madagascar, in 1718. As chapter 2 showed, this site proved to be crucial in rescuing arabica from the ravages of coffee leaf rust in the late nineteenth century.

Coffee was not grown in Hawaii until 1828 and not in Kenya, just south of its homeland in Ethiopia, until 1893. At last the tree had truly circled the globe. In both Hawaii and Kenya, missionaries brought the plants. Why not try to spread the gospel and a sobering brew at the same time?

In these early cases, it is difficult to imagine that coffee, like sugar, would have flourished without slavery or other modes of unfree labor. No one has tried to count the number of slaves, let alone the number of indigenous men, women, and children, forced to cultivate and pick coffee in the Americas and the Dutch East Indies. Surely the total would be in the tens of millions. Slavery was not abolished in Cuba until 1886 and in Brazil until 1888. Guatemalan Indians, poor and isolated from each other, were legally or illegally required to work on large estates owned by whites into the 1950s.

An exotic taste and luxury consumed in the northern hemisphere but produced on the backs of dark-skinned people in southern latitudes—this is much of the story of coffee even into recent times. Among coffee-growing lands, only Costa Rica escaped this past and its legacy, largely because the native population there perished especially quickly, leaving whites to work independently or for each other. That situation precluded the development of large plantations, a situation that in turn produced more of a sense of equality among Ticos, as Costa Ricans call themselves. The racial dimension that so often aids and extends the life of unfree labor did not arise in Costa Rica.

Wherever coffee to drink appeared, it likely made the same impression at first as in England: it was new, exotic, and afforded a taste of luxury. Café Procope in Paris featured tall mirrors, gilt everywhere, and marble tables. Viennese coffeehouses at the end of the eighteenth century often boasted of "mirrors, crystal lamps, clocks, billiard tables, porcelain as well as marble tables and armchairs." But it is not so clear that coffee everywhere stimulated wit or even conversation. Coffeehouses in Vienna featured small tables, "with many corners and niches, which created opaque walls of privacy."[59] In Austria and throughout the Hapsburg Empire of which it was a part, coffee long remained an urban pleasure. Village folk did not drink it regularly until the twentieth century. For all that the cafés of Prague, Budapest, Salzburg, and other towns became justly famous for their service and decor, the Empire's peasants long regarded coffee as a negative symbol; it was sometimes called the bankruptcy drink.[60]

Nevertheless, when coffeehouses appeared for the first time in many places, they fairly rapidly became centers of news and of social education—and, as we shall see in chapter 4, of gatherings and political discussions that disturbed the authorities. The importance of family lineage began to fade a bit in Britain in the seventeenth century relative to a new concept: wit, which referred to more than just humor. Did you have something worth saying, some item of news, perhaps? Could you say it in a lively way? Then, if you were more or less clean and well behaved, you could sit for hours in a coffeehouse and engage in conversation, even with your social betters. The *Spectator* called itself a "work which endeavours to cultivate and polish human life," to "enliven morality with wit, and to temper wit with morality."[61]

At first, our beloved drink in England—although the early houses often also served alcoholic beverages—must have been generally awful. The beans, however old to begin with, were roasted manually over a fire, in a kind of round iron chamber with a long handle used to rotate the apparatus, and then ground by hand. The uneven results were dumped into large iron cauldrons suspended over open fires. Staff poured in water and let it all simmer for hours, brewing a fairly foul concoction. The British were therefore particularly grateful that sugar began to flow into the country in large quantities during that same seventeenth century.

Vile as the brew may have been, it did allow people—overwhelmingly men, to be sure—to sit for hours, talk, exchange views, and remain sober. Here again, too much can be ascribed to coffee; it was undoubtedly a "think drink," but it was not the great soberer of Europe. After all, elaborate rules and customs regulated the drinking of alcohol before coffee arrived. A drunken merchant and his money were soon parted, and toasts were for ceremonial occasions or to seal a deal. Public drunkenness was unwelcome or outright illegal in the early modern period (roughly 1500–1789), and vomiting marked a man as unable to control himself.[62]

Yet for all of coffee's early popularity and functions in Britain, it began to yield to tea by the mid-eighteenth century. The British East India Company began to import tea from Canton on a regular basis in 1717, at just about the time that gin also became popular, as well as ruinous for the public. Tea imports to England and Wales in 1784 amounted to 16.3 million pounds, while coffee reached only 7 million pounds.[63] Tea was easier to make, and leaves could be reused by the poor. For coffee, little time and no equipment were available to put together a drink in Britain's early factories, while tea could be made quickly. The country's import tax structure also shifted to benefit the East India Company, which imported porcelain as well as tea from China. (Tea cultivation in India was still a century in the future.)

Perhaps more important in the relative, although not absolute, decline of the great British coffeehouses was the loss of several important roles to other venues and channels. Gentlemen's clubs began to draw off the upper male strata. Newspapers became available across the country, making it unnecessary to sit in a coffeehouse to read them. And the houses became old news—not exciting, let alone exotic. As Timothy Morton puts it, "Yesterday's banquet ingredient becomes today's Dunkin Donuts apple cinnamon item."[64] That is, if the exotic stays around long enough, it becomes the ordinary.

What specialty coffee has been working to accomplish in the past several decades is to make coffee exotic again, for instance by putting illustrations of lions, demons on bicycles, appealingly rusty old trucks, or charming Latin American farmers on packages. The idea is to make consumers sense in some way that the drink connects them to a distant, different place.

The journey from exotic to ordinary also depends on another important factor. While there is no question that tastes trickle down from the upper classes to ordinary folk, new products also have to be widely available and affordable to become standard in the life of any country. For Europe, that meant that real wages had to rise, which did happen in Western economies, albeit with many downturns, in the seventeenth and eighteenth centuries. The coffee trade had to be developed on a large scale through shipping and control of the crop. While commerce in beans began with Turkish or Arab traders who obtained their product from Yemen, coffee had to become a global commodity raised on plantations to reach the masses in Europe and elsewhere. In fact, I would argue, it became the first truly global product, as by the early 1700s it was grown not only in Yemen, but also in those fabled Spice Islands, and by the 1740s in the Caribbean. It was shipped from those sites to Europe and North America. When that happened and when plantations using slave labor flourished in the French colony of Saint Domingue, now Haiti, around the same time, the drink could become affordable to a large portion of the Western population. By 1789, on the eve of the French Revolution, Saint Domingue produced fully half of the world's coffee. Meanwhile, the trees kept spreading farther into Asia and Africa and farther south in Latin America. By the late nineteenth century, Brazil was—as it remains—the world's largest producer.

Most coffee moved around the world then and now is green, as already noted. What has to be done to the beans to make them into ingredients for drink? Here the industry has made immense strides since the days of tossing ground coffee into a kettle, pouring in water and bringing it to a boil, and hoping for potable results. The next section describes how far preparing coffee drinks has come since the era of the first coffeehouses.

ROASTING

Why do we roast coffee? There are two reasons: First, the beans must become brittle enough to allow grinding them. Their chemical and physical form after roasting and grinding must be such that when water is passed or forced through the grounds, it removes some of the solids into the cup. Usually, the solids amount to no more than 2 percent of the final liquor. In roasting, the microstructure of the coffee changes from dense to very porous. Don't try to grind green coffee, even as an experiment. Even if you don't ruin your grinder, you will end up with a tasteless mess if you make a cup from the grounds. Second, the chemical and physical composition of the beans must be changed by heating them, in a carefully regulated fashion, in order to develop any flavors inherent in the beans. Roast improperly, for example, by making the beans too light or too dark, and the flavors will not develop well.

At least eight hundred volatile organic compounds (VOCs) can be found in a cup of good brewed arabica coffee; some observers put the figure at more than a thousand. Wine may have four hundred. A VOC, sometimes just called a volatile, is any carbon compound that interacts rapidly with the atmosphere. Once exposed to air, liquid formaldehyde quickly turns to gas, for instance (don't worry—there isn't any formaldehyde in coffee). A volatile evaporates quickly upon exposure to air, especially to the oxygen in it. Green coffee starts with about two hundred VOCs, and they are not especially volatile, so it is easy to see just how much the beans change when roasted. Although much research is under way to determine how the compounds produced in roasting affect taste, we still know little about the relationship.

Dissolved solids in the cup are what gives coffee its taste, while VOCs, as the name suggests, contribute to aroma. Body is more the product of solids, oils, and suspended particles.[65]

How does a coffee roaster (a person) use a coffee roaster (a machine or a simpler device) to get flavors out of green, unroasted beans? Before delving into the basics of all that, note that not all cooked coffee is roasted. In many areas where coffee grows, it may be fried or baked. Frying results in uneven development and usually does not allow heat to penetrate adequately to the interior of the beans before they become dark brown or burnt on the outside. Baking—holding the temperature steady as the beans cook—is a serious error. Flavors are flattened and/or become grassy, straw-like, or otherwise unpleasant in the cup. In the coffee business, roasting means to keep the temperature in your machine rising constantly throughout the roast, however small the increments might be. This is rule number one; more injunctions follow below.

Small growers are often reduced to preparing third-rate coffee from their own beans. First-grade coffee goes for export, second-grade is for use inside the country—although this is changing in a number of places—and third-grade coffee is for consumption on the farm. There are still small farmers who have never tasted their own coffee, because they must sell it all to stay afloat. Where little money is available for anything fancy, a condition that characterizes millions of small producers, the low-quality beans will be fried on top of the stove. Put a little fat of some sort in a pan, heat, pour in the beans, stir until they turn brown, grind somehow, brew, and serve. For the most part, this method produces some pretty terrible beverages, at least in my experience.

True, the Ethiopian coffee ceremony—which is not especially old, and probably appeared for tourists in the twentieth century—involves frying the beans, grinding them on the spot with a mortar and pestle, then going through a formal serving pattern, first to the eldest or most honored guest, then down the pecking order. While this is fun to see and try, the liquor leaves something to be desired.

An alternative long in common use was to roast—again, really, to bake—green coffee in an oven. This approach was typical in nineteenth-century American kitchens. Today's low cost, do-it-yourself methods rely on popcorn poppers, hair dryers, maybe even flame-and-shake apparatuses put together in the basement. But all of the methods just mentioned can have problems: They probably lack adequate ways to regulate the temperature, certainly not quickly, or to change the direction and force of air flow over and through the beans. So these methods, while they can transform green beans to brown ones, may heat them unevenly and flatten any flavor notes that might have been inherent in the coffee. If you have rigged up a DIY kit that does well, more power to you. But in general there is a big step up from frying, cooking in the oven, or just blowing hot air through the beans, to a machine that effectively heats the beans while having the capacity to change the temperature and air flow, and at the same time agitating the beans so that they heat evenly and all the way through.

Roasting well means developing a profile, a time, temperature, and air flow pattern, that allows the operator to (1) "charge" (dump) the beans into a roaster when it has reached a certain internal temperature; (2) let the temperature of the beans fall to a certain level; (3) then, until the roast is finished, keep the temperature inside the device rising steadily; and (4) have a way to get the finished beans out of the roaster quickly and to cool them back to room temperature within 3–4 minutes. Medium-size and large roasters, on the order of 50 or more kilos per batch, have quenching systems that spray a mist of water on the beans as they pour out of the machine, cooling them quite quickly. Smaller machines have perforated cooling trays with rotating paddles; fresh air is drawn up through the tray and the beans as they are spread around either by hand or by a paddle.

Professional sample roasters, used in specialty operations to prepare small amounts of coffee in order to determine optimal profiles, can work fine at home, as long as they are safely set up. That includes making sure electrical circuits and outlets are right for the machine, propane or natural gas brought to it is safely supplied, any tanks involved are placed outside the home, and the gases and hot air from roasting are properly vented. Many a home roaster has had to put the whole assembly outdoors, depending on reactions from domestic partners. It is definitely a bad idea to keep a propane tank inside a dwelling; at the least, that may void your home fire insurance. Be sure you can vent properly before spending serious money, up to thousands of dollars in the U.S., for a sophisticated home or sample roaster.

Early roasting techniques used closed or open pans over fires. Throughout the nineteenth century, many refinements appeared. Coffee museums display old wood- or coal-fired devices that at first had to be hand cranked or even animal powered in order to keep the beans moving and not burn them.

Large commercial roasters in use by the early nineteenth century were loaded by hand; at the end of a roast, heavy, hot cylinders had to be pulled out of the heating chamber in order to dump the coffee. Then in 1864, the American Jabez Burns patented a roaster with flanges inside a rotating drum, so that the finished coffee would be pushed out of the machine. By 1881, Burns roasters featured a door at the front that could be opened at the end of a roast, whereupon the flanges would push the coffee out into a cooling tray. There was even a hole in

A "pot roaster," circa 1750, Badilatti Museum, Zuoz, Switzerland. The roaster used wood or coal for heat. During the roast, workers had to agitate the beans by lifting the roaster handles and shaking the whole device. At the end of a roast, the beans were scooped out with a small shovel.
Photo by Robert Thurston

the machine through which small samples could be drawn throughout the roast, to check on the color of the beans; today this arrangement is common, and the device used to take samples is called a trier or trowel. Typically it has a concave metal part that sits inside the roaster, with a wooden handle on the outside.

All of the nineteenth-century developments marked great strides in controlling the roast, not to mention taking some of the intense heat off the men who operated the machines. Still, roasting devices remained seriously inefficient in their use of fuel, and a lot of cool air had to be constantly introduced into the main chamber to prevent the coffee from burning.

What remained to do, then, was to shift from coal or wood to electricity or gas, for steadier and more controllable heat; to put small perforations in the roasting cylinder, which improved air flow; to refine the flanges and baffles, also for better air flow; and to improve the way heat and air were delivered to the beans. Afterburners or converters have become available, and are sometimes required by law if the roaster is large enough, to deal with the particulate emissions that accompany roasting and to render harmless any nasty gaseous emissions from the roaster. At the same time, chaff—the bits of silverskin that inevitably remain on the beans after hulling—blows off and separates from the beans at a certain point in the roast. Chaff, light brown, very light and fluffy, is typically drawn off into a collector, which must be emptied often. Don't do that right at the end of a roast, when the chaff is hot! And never empty hot chaff into a waste container, especially a wooden barrel. I have seen a photo of that mistake, which resulted in a terrible fire and heavy damage to a roastery. Stefan Diedrich, a roaster manufacturer, remarked to a group I was in that no industry is as tolerant of fire as coffee. Well, there is no reason to have a fire in a shop. Much depends on proper cleaning and regular maintenance of equipment.

Heat from electricity or combusting gas can now be delivered to ceramic plates, which efficiently use radiant heat and transfer it to the beans. Finally, computers began to appear in the 1990s to keep track of roasts, so that they can be tweaked for better development and can be duplicated by another person or an automated system. Roasting time has dropped with all these advances, down from 60 minutes to 30 with the Jabez Burns products and then to 15 minutes or less with today's machines. "Flash" roasters exist that can make the beans brown in as little as 2 minutes. I would taste such coffee before buying.

A small Diedrich (can be pronounced "Died Rich") roaster. Visible are the wooden handle of the trier, the window through which to watch changes in bean color, the end of a temperature probe going into the drum, and, at the far left side, the air flow control lever. The lever directs air through the cooling bin in phase 1 of the roast, air through the bin and through the drum in phase 2, air only through the drum in phase 3.

Photo by Robert Thurston

Today's roasters operate on one of two principles in heating beans. The majority of roasters have a drum, positioned to rotate either on a vertical or a horizontal axis; the other principle is to push hot air through the beans, in what is naturally called a hot air roaster—or, more obscurely, a fluid bed roaster. Whether the roasting chamber is vertical or horizontal, the hot air drawn into it both heats the beans and agitates them. Drum roasters suck in air, while air roasters blow it into a column.

The beans are heated by conduction, meaning direct contact with a hot surface; by convection, as hot air moves among the beans; and by radiation, for instance, from the ceramic plates just mentioned. A drum roaster typically cooks largely by conduction and convection, although much more from the former. An air roaster heats the beans almost entirely by convection.

Today's "clean" roasters do not need afterburners. These machines may, however, be equipped with environmentally friendly, if somewhat more energy-greedy, add-ons such as catalytic oxidizers. These work somewhat the way catalytic converters do on cars, by trapping undesirable particles. Newer roasters can also recirculate some of the hot air from the roasting chamber back into it, again saving energy. Or the whole apparatus might be rigged to heat the roastery itself in cold weather. Recent advances also allow operators to quickly change the temperature in drums and the speed of their rotation.

Small but reliable sample roasters can handle as little as 30 grams at a time, while the biggest industrial machines take up many square meters of space and can roast as much as 5,000 kilograms an hour. The pipes that deliver green coffee to such monsters and remove gases from them look like the wildest imaginings of children's book illustrators.

There is something quite positive to be said for roasters in, say, the 7–80 kilo per batch range, as they are more likely to be operated by a skilled and experienced person who is dedicated to producing good coffee. Anyone who cooks up 5,000 kilos of coffee in one hour is not using especially fine beans to begin with. At that size, the operation is set up for commodity coffee.

If the coffee has absolutely no character to begin with, it doesn't much matter how it is roasted. Roasting can only bring out, never improve upon, the inherent qualities of beans. And the darker the roast, the less it matters how the coffee got there or what the coffee beans were in the first place. At some point, the taste in the cup of a dark roast is predominantly the darkness itself (yes, you can taste darkness in this sense), not any qualities the beans may have had. If you like dark roasts, fine, although I hope that you don't like them too dark. If the beans are black and have a lot of visible, physical oil on the surface, in what is sometimes called French roast, and (darker yet) Italian roast, the taste in the cup will be somewhat bitter and harsh. Aroma volatiles quickly dissipate from such roasts. Yet coffees cooked to a dark brown or black state still please many palates. Often the taste is described as bold or strong, words which in practice have little meaning. To my mind, the word "strong" should apply only to the ratio of water to ground coffee used to make any coffee liquor.

With many of my colleagues in specialty coffee, I favor light to medium roasts. To coax out or reveal flavor in quality beans, it's necessary to take real care in roasting them. In the best roasteries, that means figuring out a proper roast profile for every lot of green coffee, and even through the life of a 60-kilo bag, if some weeks have elapsed since the last roast from that bag. This is where experience and sample roasters come in; the small amounts of coffee they can handle make it possible to do a number of sample roasts without burning up a lot of coffee and money. It is also useful to test for density and humidity in the beans, using small machines which cost mere hundreds of dollars each.

Rough guidelines exist for roasting certain kinds of beans. Sumatrans, with their heavy body, can take dark roast better than, say, Costa Ricans. Gesha, mainly from Panama and Colombia, with some now from Costa Rica, needs a light roast. Go even a little dark and the floral notes in particular are destroyed in this coffee. Some coffees best express their potential with a relatively long finish time in the roaster, reaching a low final temperature, as roasts go. An example in our shop is Ethiopian Yirgacheffe (which, to be sure, can vary a lot from farm to farm or year to year). Once we get these beans close to the first crack, when water content in them turns to steam and escapes with noticeable noise through the cell walls, we turn the gas down and let the roast continue for a minute or slightly more past the crack. Maximum time in the roaster is under 13 minutes, and the final temperature will not be above 385°F.

In contrast, a dark roast will go into a second, less audible crack, when caramelization turns to carbonization—the beans are literally burning—and may end after 15 or more minutes at 420–440°F. Keep in mind that these are examples

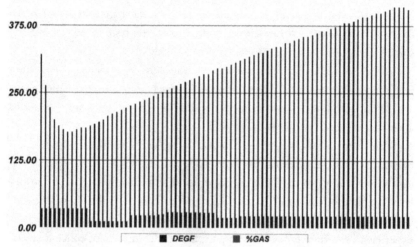

Here is the profile of a roast we did recently of a Honduran coffee. Nothing fancy; we just wanted the temperature in the drum to keep rising, slowly, which we accomplished by regulating the gas supply and the air flow through the machine. We barely took this roast past first crack.
Courtesy of Oxford Coffee Company

from my shop, with a small roaster, and that different roasters behave differently, especially in temperature and air flow controls. In another machine, the final temperature might be quite a bit higher. I give time and temperature examples here for my operation merely to show the range of difference in roasting.

A pound (455g) of medium-roasted coffee will be composed of 2,800–4,725 coffee beans (depending on their density).[66] One bean roasted medium usually amounts to about 0.1g in weight. From a pound of roasted beans, it might be possible to get 6,825 grams of coffee liquor, at a ratio of 15 times water to coffee. Then, by my rule that 240 grams of liquor amounts to an 8-ounce (by volume) cup, the pound of beans will yield 28 to 30 cups of coffee to drink.

❧

Many a smaller operation has proceeded, with good results, without the extra and expensive paraphernalia required to test density and humidity. It is more important for high-class roasters to follow a standard mantra: roast and cup, roast and cup. This means that a sample roast is prepared and cupped right away or a day later; with enough experience, the roaster-cuppers (far from all are Q cuppers) can then imagine ways the roast can be improved. More sample roasts, as many as twenty, may follow. Roasters consider how the charge temperature might be set higher or lower. Then once the beans are in the roaster, would it be better to bring the machine's internal temperature up quickly or slowly?

Roaster operators watch their bean probe (a thin metal rod located inside the drum at the point where beans tend to congregate) and another probe that gives the temperature inside the drum. There should be a manometer on the machine to check gas flow, or a gauge of some sort that regulates electrical energy going into the chamber. The bean probe tells what is happening to the beans; the changes in their internal temperature are regulated by changing the gas or electricity flow, as well as air flow. There is certainly some science to all this, as roasters need to understand in a basic way what is happening to the beans as they cook. But in my view, and in conversations with numerous roasters, coaxing maximum flavors from beans is more a matter of art and sensory perception. Sight, smell, and sound from the roasting chamber all come into play.

Avoid baking, of course. But how fast should the temperature rise—to use a fancy term, what is the ΔT, the change in temperature over time? The highly experienced roaster Scott Rao has issued a second "commandment": The ΔT or "rate of rise" must always decrease throughout the roast. To be clear, the *temperature* inside the roasting machine must always rise, but the *rate* at which it rises must constantly be reduced, in Rao's view. That practice allows heat to penetrate the beans thoroughly and thus to cook them all the way through. For Rao, this is essential for the full "development" of a roast; that is, to bring out the flavors locked in green beans.[67] That still leaves several questions: How fast should the coffee be brought to first crack, then to second crack—if somehow it is necessary to go that far? What should the length of the roast be, and what final temperature is best? All of that depends not only on the variety of coffee being roasted, but, again, on its density, internal humidity, bean size, and conditions of storage. Having green coffee delivered from a truck in a Wisconsin winter and dumping some of it right away into a roaster is a bad idea, for example. Storing green coffee for any length of time in Florida in a room without climate control will likewise affect the way the beans act in the roaster and how the final product will taste in the cup.

Another experiment, which requires a special request to a roaster in many cases: Ask for the same variety of beans roasted differently. Choose something you like in the first place, and get samples roasted light, medium, and dark. You only need a few hundred grams of each. What are the differences you can taste? Be nice to the roaster and pay extra for the trouble. Many roasters are happy to hold tasting sessions in which one variety of bean is roasted three different ways, or three beans are roasted the same way, or one roast is prepared in three different ways, for example, French press, pour-over, Aeropress®. Seek and ye shall find such tastings, maybe even cuppings, in various shops.

    That is more or less how green beans turn brown in roasting and hopefully express their flavor notes. What, more precisely, is happening to the beans as they roast? They go through a number of chemical and physical changes, some of them fairly violent. The interior of the beans becomes a "mini-reactor" during roasting.[68] Basically, we are speaking of the formation of or changes in sugars and acids in the coffee. The sugars are transformed as they caramelize, which means that they become somewhat gooey and change structure. As that happens, several kinds of acids either appear or are changed in form. No sugar in the cup, no sweetness, of course. No acids worth mentioning, no development of all sorts of flavors and aromas. It is all well and good to keep track of time and temperature in the roast, to watch for color changes, and to smell the beans. Make that ΔT decrease throughout the roast, if you follow Scott Rao's rule. Maybe keep the time after first crack to no more than 20–25 percent of the total roast time. But it is the whole roast profile that really matters.

Charging beans into a roaster's chamber makes its internal temperature drop sharply, because the beans are at room temperature. As the beans begin to absorb heat, the first change is a Maillard reaction: "an amino acid (a component of protein) reacts with carbohydrates (often sugars)."[69] Simply put, this is a browning process; the same thing occurs, without the application of heat, to an apple cut open and left out. Maillard reactions cause the outside of baked bread or of a grilled steak to turn brown. Nature is beginning to lock some flavors, particularly caramel and chocolate, into the material. What the "Maillard reaction contributes to roasted coffee is complexity of flavor—through the types of sugars, the amount of perceived acidity, and the structure of the viscosity. The Maillard reaction is responsible for nothing short of the development of coffee's essential sensory character."[70] Keep in mind that the reaction continues through the roast until the coffee is dumped to cool.

As the beans heat, they will first actually turn yellow, owing to the degradation of chlorophyll. Then with more time and heat, the beans turn light brown, and finally brown or (gross!) black. As that progression takes place, the beans give off an array of smells. When yellow, the coffee smells grassy. A roast dumped too soon, an all-too-common mistake in the rush to produce light roasts over the past few decades, retains grassy notes in the cup.

Caramelization proceeds in the beans at the same time. Long chains of carbohydrates break down into sugars, while existing sugars change in composition or turn into acids. The caramelization of sucrose produces acetic acid (vinegar), enough of which will give citrus notes in the cup. In the early part of a roast, the beans are endothermic—they absorb heat. At first crack, they temporarily become exothermic—they give off heat. If the beans are taken to second crack, when CO_2 builds up within cells and suddenly escapes, causing breakage and another, quieter noise, they are again exothermic for a short time. At second crack, carbonization begins. Oil soon extrudes to the surface of the beans. Any moisture left in the coffee disappears.

It is a myth that dark roasts reduce the amount of caffeine in the beans; it stays relatively stable no matter what the roast. In fact, dark coffee may have higher levels of caffeine because of the beans' larger size—they always expand during roasting, the more so the darker they are—and because they have more surface area than lighter roasts. As the beans darken, they lose more water and liquidity in general; they become lighter in weight. Therefore the amount of caffeine rises relative to the weight of the beans.

Of the volatile compounds that result from all this, trigonelline is one of the more important. It is a bitter alkaloid (pH value is greater than 7) that—we don't understand how, as is true of so much coffee chemistry—helps produce pleasant aromas. The proportion of trigonelline in arabica is on average about two times higher than in robusta. Arabica also has some 60 percent more lipid content than robusta. For lipids, think fatty acids—for example, cholesterol and triglycerides. But fear not: most coffee will not raise your cholesterol level. Chapter 3 discusses this issue. Lipids, which don't change much during roasting due to their high melting points, help with body in the cup.

Chlorogenic acids (CGA) are among the most important compounds to survive roasting, even though their presence in the beans may decrease by 50 percent as the beans are heated. Coffee has by far the largest concentration of CGA of any plant, with robusta leading at about twice the content of arabica. The acids produced or that remain through the roast are mostly formic, acetic, and caffeic. These are long molecules of different oxygen and hydrogen combinations. It's in the CGAs that one of coffee's most valuable ingredients for health lies: the antioxidants. Roasting dark can severely reduce the CGAs, making the coffee harsher and leaving fewer antioxidants in the cup. But so far, research has not focused on whether people drink light or dark roasts, so next to nothing is known about the health benefits of drinking either. We do know that if coffee is ground just after roasting, 26–59 percent of the carbon dioxide (and undoubtedly other volatiles) will be released immediately.

Not all the recent discoveries about coffee are positive. Acrylamide, a cancer-causing agent, is a by-product of roasting. In the cup, there is not enough of it to do you any harm. Chapter 4 looks at acrylamide in more depth.

MAKING COFFEE TO DRINK

Every coffee drinker has a favorite method of making liquor. Infusion and cold brew use somewhat coarse grinds, although there is no reason to use extra-coarse grind for a (French) press pot. It's only necessary to have the grind size be larger than the holes in the plunger screen, so that few or no particles pass through the screen into the liquor.

Vacuum pots—please don't say siphon, because they don't work that way—are always crowd pleasers. They have two vessels; water is poured into the bottom one, and a tube leads down into the water from the top chamber. A heat source sits under the bottom vessel. As the water boils, it is drawn or pushed into the top part. Then medium-grind coffee is poured into the top and stirred well. Now the heat is cut off; as the apparatus cools a bit, it draws the liquor down into the bottom chamber, which always looks like magic. The liquor is smooth, if perhaps somewhat lacking in subtlety.

Whatever the method, except espresso, it usually helps to stir the coffee once, as the water is poured on. That is to make sure that all the grounds are exposed to water. Channeling occurs when the water goes through only part of the grounds, making the liquor underextracted (more on extraction below) and unappealing.

Using a dripper and filter, whether paper—bleached or not—or perhaps metal, is an easy, simple, and effective method for making brewed coffee. Many filters are now bleached using oxygen, so the environmental concerns of a few years ago about the use of nasty chemicals to do the bleaching have mostly disappeared. In any event, be sure to rinse the filters, especially unbleached ones, with very hot water before actually putting in the grounds to make a cup. Rinsing not only takes out almost all taste that a filter may have, it prepares a cup or carafe better by heating it a little. Be sure to throw out that rinse water before going farther! Both used grounds and filters can be composted.

Here's a mildly fanatical but not especially time-consuming way to make pour-over coffee: put a container of some sort on a scale accurate to a tenth of a gram. Such scales are not expensive and can be useful for other purposes in the kitchen. When you get to actually pouring water onto the grounds—not yet!—try my ratio of 15:1 or 16:1 water to coffee. Tare the container back to zero on the scale. Add the beans to get your desired weight—for example, 16 grams, which will make a fairly large cup once you have added water to bring the total weight to 240 grams. Not yet! Grind

the beans while bringing water to a boil in a goose-neck kettle. The neck allows you to direct the water exactly where you want it and to pour a little at a time.

Attention! Is your water "clean"? Some mineral content is necessary to make any coffee liquor; so far, no one is quite sure why. Distilled water won't work, but hard water is no good either. If water from your tap is not pretty low in mineral content, you should either soften it somehow with a home system or buy jugs of water. A home water filtration system, especially a reverse osmosis (R/O) one, is a great idea. At the least, get one of the plastic jugs with changeable filters.

Once you have good water, you may proceed. Put the paper (preferred) or metal filter of your choice into the dripper cone or top of a glass coffee maker. Rinse the filter, pour out that water, and place the dripper with wet filter on top of your cup. Put cup and filter on top of the scale, tare it out again, then pour in the ground coffee. You do that to recheck the weight of the grounds. Now wet the grounds with water just off the boil, enough to get all the coffee soaked. Wait 20–25 seconds. Then pour about one-third of the remaining water onto the grounds. Aim for three pours of the water. Watch what you are doing by keeping an eye on the scale. All this is not a waste of time; you could be reading War and Peace *or betting on football between pours. Good beans and simple but effective equipment plus a little time and care make excellent coffee.*

Cold brew devices use slow drips of water through the grounds. For this method too, the grind should be fairly coarse. Cold water and ice go into a top chamber, and a valve regulates the drips of water through the grounds. Wait four to eight hours, and the result is a pleasantly smooth cold coffee usually served over ice. Cold water cannot leach out as much soluble material from the beans, so the caffeine content of coffee made this way will be somewhat lower than with hot water extraction. Lately cold brew with nitrogen pumped in, for a creamier and richer texture, has become popular. Cold brew extract and canned nitro brew are available in many stores. However, some folks are quite happy with yesterday's hot coffee kept overnight in a refrigerator and poured over ice. Since the ice will melt in the drink, it's good to start with somewhat stronger coffee. Summer calls for iced coffee, but don't neglect the hot stuff on a warm day.

In the past few decades, a sometimes quiet and sometimes showy sea change in the way we make and drink coffee has rolled around the world. Who in

America or most of Europe had heard of a latte in, say, 1985? By the way, "latte" means milk in Italian, while caffè latte means espresso with steamed and foamed milk. But we have not gone completely Italian in English-speaking countries. Be careful what you order while visiting Italy—although in the cities, baristas are used to Americans and probably others abusing their language. Italians don't drink milky coffee after lunch, as they think it will do battle in your stomach with the tomatoes you have invariably just eaten. They also consider lattes to be for women or people who are ill. Italian style is still for the most part to belly up to the bar and order a single or double espresso, toss it down quickly, and leave. Or sit at a table, have the waiter come over, and pay a good deal more for the same drinks.

The Swedes don't care about any of that; they have "latte dads," men who, because of the country's generous paternity leave policy, have free time to meet with their pals and drink milky coffee. For the ultimate in barista-made milk beverages, go to Australia and order a babycino—right, no coffee in the cup at all. Originally developed so that customers could give their small children something nice to drink, the idea has spread a little to adults.

Some general rules, not exactly enforced by anyone, apply to making espresso and cappuccino. Espresso coffee, which doesn't have to be roasted dark anymore, and which is the subject of endless blending and single-origin experiments, needs to be ground to the consistency of fine sand. Grind coffee to powder and you are ready to make Mediterranean coffee—called Turkish, Greek, Armenian, and so on, depending on where you are. Ground espresso, in the range of 18–22 grams for a double shot, goes into a portafilter, which has a metal basket with small holes, and is tamped down pretty hard. The portafilter is hooked into a machine, which should take 20–30 seconds at 9 bars of pressure (9 times air pressure at sea level) to extract a double shot. That is 2 fluid ounces in the U.S., almost 60 milliliters elsewhere. The light-brown foam on top, crema (Italian for cream), actually has a function: it helps hold flavor in the drink. Espresso can be wonderfully sweet, have layers of flavor, plenty of body, and a fine, long finish.

Home espresso machines can work well, but they usually cannot sustain 9 bars over a number of shots, although they may produce much higher pressure for a few shots. Watch out for lime scale in any home coffeemaker; if you have hard water, soften and filter it, and from time to time run a solution of citric acid through your machine. Citric acid is available in the home canning section of almost any big grocery store.

A *ristretto* ("restricted" in Italian) is a particularly strong espresso made by using a finer grind, tamping harder, putting more coffee into the portafilter—or some combination of those steps—and extracted in less time. This drink is for the hard core. Cappuccinos are traditionally made with one-third espresso, one-third steamed milk, and one-third foamed milk, which can be bubbly. A good-looking cap has foam in a small dome above the lip of the cup.

Lattes, on the other hand, can be prepared in various ways. Lattes should have milk foamed to the texture of thick paint. They may be as strong as cappuccinos, in terms of the liquor:milk ratio, or as weak as one-seventh coffee. While some especially cool baristas can make latte art with any kind of milk, and even somehow do that on top of a cappuccino, most of us more hapless bar folk can do rosettes and so forth much better with whole milk than with 2% or skim. If you like almond, soy, rice, or any other non-dairy milk, don't expect much in the way of art on top of your drink. As for flat whites, invented in Australia, they seem to me to be another form of latte, except that the layer of foam should be even thinner.

Dry caps have more foamed and less steamed milk. Wet is the opposite. *Macchiato*, notwithstanding its perversion by some big chains, means "marked" or "spotted" in Italian. That involves foaming a little milk and putting dots of it on top of espresso. Adding chocolate should be specified as adding chocolate, not called "mocha." That word came from a port in Yemen; in the not-so-old days, Mocha-Java was a brand name that had essentially no meaning; there was never an indication of where the coffee came from.

The noisy part of all this is the many competitions, from latte art to best cold brew, held at coffee trade shows. Contestants in making pour-over coffee—a technique well over a hundred years old—spend a lot of time separating the good grinds from "fines," small particles not ground well that almost invariably also exit from any grinder. But even in everyday work in a good shop, controlling water temperature throughout a pour, changing the grind and water pressure when pulling an espresso shot, and measuring everything carefully, is the route to good results. This is a different world from the 1960s way of making coffee. Percolators were brutal devices, as they kept heating the coffee and recycling it through the grounds. Bad, coarse ground coffee in, produced a hot thin liquid out, with hints of burnt steel as flavor.

A highly useful tool that helps to guide baristas as well as to let roasters know what's happening with their coffee is the refractometer. This instrument is available in small, hand-held versions that can be linked to a smartphone or computer. Place a few drops of brewed coffee or espresso in a small indentation in the refractometer, and it will tell you the percentage of total dissolved solids (tds) in the coffee. The device will also register the extraction yield, how much of the material in the beans has been removed into the liquor. Right away, roasters and baristas know if the coffee they are making is over- or underextracted or close to being just right. Underextracted means that not enough flavor has been removed from the ground coffee by water; such coffee will be weak and undeveloped in flavor notes. The liquor will be sour, not to be confused with acidity or sparkle on the tongue.[71] Sour is unpleasant, but acidity—if not too noticeable, to the detriment of other characteristics in the cup—is a pleasant sensation. Again, think champagne, although in coffee the effect is not nearly as powerful as in sparkling wine. Underdeveloped brew lacks sweetness, has a short finish at best, and may taste slightly salty.

It used to be said in Italy that the sign of a good barista was that he (always he at first) was missing some front teeth. That was because the old lever machines needed their handles pulled down with some force, to be held in place, as we have seen, by compressing large springs. But if the barista was busy with several machines, he might turn back to the first one just in time to have the spring release a lever into his mouth. With the virtual eclipse in coffeehouses of lever machines—although you can still buy them, and they can work very well—the toothless barista pretty much disappeared.

How can you spot a good roaster (person) today? If you can get close enough, look for a scarred place on the left hand, where one too many times the operator has allowed the trier to touch the flesh while she looked at and sniffed the beans during a roast, as often as every few seconds toward the end of a batch. Better yet might be a little scar tissue at the end of the nose, from getting it too close to hot beans. More than a few roasters say that they judge the progress and proper end point of a roast by the smell of the beans.

Overextracted coffee will taste "strong," in the sense of having a lot of impact in the mouth, but will have taken so much from the grounds that flavor notes are pretty much blotted out. The coffee just won't do much beyond that first hit; no sense of richness is present. The liquor will be astringent, as though something was trying to dry out your mouth.

There is no need to get a lot of fancy equipment to make good coffee at home. Good beans, a simple dripper cone and filters or a French press, a good burr grinder, and you are in business to please yourself and your friends. Why buy a fancy machine to make regular coffee that may clog with lime scale and fail to keep an even temperature? Espresso is different; to make good liquor at home, I think spending $600 or more for a sturdy machine, without any fancy bells and whistles, is necessary. Beyond those ingredients, the road goes on forever, through more toys, effort, and money.

Meanwhile, seek out a good coffeehouse with friendly, down-to-earth baristas. Around the country, even in smaller cities and university towns, there are excellent opportunities to go to coffee tastings and talks. As I used to tell my students, there is no such thing as a stupid question. There are, however, ignorant questions—but it's the job of the coffee specialist to turn those into insightful queries and answer them.

In a well-known one-liner, the French writer Antoine de Saint-Exupéry said, "It is the time you have wasted on your rose that makes your rose so important." Maybe that applies to coffee as well. But of course taking a little time and care is not wasting the minutes, when the result is a sweet, subtle drink. Like roses, beans vary almost endlessly. Compare a typical Costa Rican to a single-origin Sumatran, and wander through the great coffees from Africa and the rest of Latin America. If you want to try something "wilder," as the industry puts it, meaning somewhat unpredictable but often with strikingly good tastes, go for monsooned Indian beans or some from Papua New Guinea. Be sure to include some naturals in your selection, to see what kinds of extra sweetness and flavors might emerge from them.

You can have excellent coffee year 'round, while the roses will wilt quickly. But be of good cheer in any event, for you can put used coffee grounds around your roses and have it all.

4

Coffee and Health, Social and Personal

Coffee has never been a mere beverage.[1]

VitaCup Has a Mission: Create a Vitamin Infused Brew for You. . . . VitaCup brings you a tastier, easy vitamin delivery method to jumpstart your day.[2]

First, a big caveat for this part of the book; I am a doctor, but not that kind of doctor. So please talk to your physician if you have concerns about your health and coffee. What I can do with the subject is to scour and report on the studies done by qualified, serious scientific researchers. Many such studies have been done in the past few years, with new ones appearing regularly. The news is almost entirely positive: Coffee is good for you. Yet every body is different chemically, and reactions to coffee and caffeine will vary a lot from person to person.

That coffee has never been "a mere beverage" should be abundantly clear by now, but what Ralph Hattox meant was that coffee has raised social and political issues almost from the moment it was first served in Middle Eastern coffeehouses. VitaCup's claims point to another controversial—although much less so recently—part of coffee's daily life: health concerns. These two sides of coffee consumption have been closely intertwined, to the point that it has frequently been hard to separate social health or well-being from questions of personal health.

Why anyone would need extra vitamins "infused"—which must mean simply added—in coffee must remain a mystery. If you need to take vitamins, that's fine, but do be aware that taking extra vitamins may not benefit you at all; vitamin and other dietary supplements may in fact bring health risks.[3] All coffee is already packed with "melanoidins: potent anti-oxidants," which help fight or ward off some types of cancer, as we shall see. Antioxidants can be 25 percent of brewed coffee's composition.[4]

VitaCup is trying to jump on the bandwagon of promoting pills, "natural" drinks, detoxification, eating the "right" foods, and just plain mysticism about good health. Its coffee, the company claims, helps combat depression and assists in weight loss.[5] Maybe it also makes you wealthy and sexy. Americans appear to be concerned if not obsessed about their health and body image on a vast scale, or on a home scale, and claims like VitaCup's play to fears that something has gone terribly wrong with our food and drink. For coffee, that idea is nothing new.

HOW COFFEE BROUGHT SOCIAL AND POLITICAL DISRUPTION TO THE WORLD

The charge that coffee is bad for people and society was flung against it when it first appeared in a number of lands. To be sure, coffee and its attendant social life did upset traditional life in certain ways, and coffeehouses and consumption drew suspicion from authorities. But let us back up for a moment. It is a myth that before the arrival of coffee and tea in Europe, people were partly or completely drunk and sleepy much of the time, because they had beer soup for breakfast and beer or ale to drink all day. While drinking water in many towns and even in the countryside was understood early on to be dangerous, and we should never underestimate European drunkenness, it is not true that inebriated workers were forever falling off castle and cathedral walls as they tried to build them. But as chapter 3 showed, Europeans, and of course many other peoples, did experience coffee and tea as something new, producing unprecedented sensations and effects on mind and body. For that reason alone, coffee was suspect. Were those effects good for people or were they dangerous? When coffee had a noticeable impact on people's wits, and then they used their sharpened minds in public places and discussed news and politics openly, also a new development with coffeehouses, the more socially and politically conservative part of the population, especially among the authorities, sometimes took offense.

Coffeehouses can be called an early and important social medium. Where could anyone get news or have serious discussions about anything before coffeehouses opened? No newspapers existed, nor did places for meeting others and talking about local and world affairs. People could gather at churches, temples, and mosques, but they usually went there to hear from a religious authority, not to have conversations with that official source or long conversations with others in attendance. The marketplace in any town was a meeting site, but for people no higher in society than the upper rungs of the lower classes. Servants and workers, not well-to-do people, went to the markets or to wells. Serious conversations took place in private dwellings, but the participants were very likely drawn from the same social class as the host. Taverns and inns existed in many countries and were often sites of social life and business transactions. But they were not known for social intercourse unless specific groups, for example, guild members, met there, keeping interaction among themselves. Thus the coffeehouses, with their psychoactive drink, represented something previously unknown for public places and gatherings. As new sites of talk, they were often disturbing to authorities who had been used to closely controlled discussions of policy and current events.

The first known attempt to outlaw coffee dates from Mecca in 1511, but the case must have arisen from earlier objections to coffee and the new kind of social life it engendered. The city's council of Muslim scholars and legal authorities, the *ulema*, investigated reports of men congregating at night and drinking a hot brew. When the charge of unwanted activities came before the clerics, they quickly prohibited the gatherings. After hearing testimony from several witnesses, including two doctors who denounced coffee as a beverage harmful to health, the ulema also prohibited coffee itself.

In part, the Mecca decision quickly failed. Clerical authorities in Cairo, who were at the time superior to those in Mecca—both cities were then ruled by the Ottoman Turks—agreed that gathering to drink coffee should be forbidden. But they pronounced the beverage itself acceptable. In fact, the Meccan religious officials who pushed through the edicts against coffee were soon removed from their positions, although it is unclear that their dismissal had anything to do with their broad ruling against the beverage. The physicians who argued against coffee were eventually executed in Cairo by a method in vogue at the time: They were cut in half at the waist.[6] Again, it is not certain that their punishment was related to the earlier incident involving coffee. Yet the fact that they had expressed an opinion unwelcome in Cairo must have played a role in their deaths.

The Ottoman Turkish rulers of the Middle East at the time continued to issue conflicting or ineffective judgments about coffee and coffeehouses. By the 1530s, "coffee-drinking . . . spread in both Damascus and Aleppo . . . and was associated with unbecoming behavior. Because of this, it was banned time and again."[7] The repeated edicts indicate repeated failure to outlaw coffee. Muhammad al-Husayni, chief Ottoman judge in Aleppo, banned coffee in the city in 1543. He also asked Sultan Suleiman the Magnificent (1494–1566), based in Istanbul, to impose the ban in all Ottoman-controlled territory, which he did in 1546. According to one account, in 1554 Suleiman imposed a tax on coffee—which people were obviously still drinking, despite the 1546 order—in an effort to limit its consumption to the well-off.[8]

The problem with coffee in these Middle Eastern cases appears to have been much more the new behavior associated with consuming it than the drink itself. To follow this story, it is worth looking at the background of the Arabic word for coffee, "qahwa" or "qahua." One source identifies it as used for several centuries by "mystics" in the region to "symbolize divine love."[9] Other specialists give its etymology as a word for wine, which is of course forbidden in Islam. Still other dictionaries and articles discuss qahwa as coming from a root meaning "repugnant" and "should be avoided." That denunciation is related to the Arabic verb to "make dull," as in blunting the edge of a knife. The idea is that coffee dulled the appetite,[10] an undesired outcome in the population.

When Muslim clerics spoke against coffee or tried to ban it outright, they "mentioned dissolute behavior" in coffeehouses. Suleiman ordered five coffee establishments operating in Jerusalem to close in 1565, in yet another attempt to control the drink and its social life, calling them "the meeting place of rascals." For Turkish civil authorities and leading Muslim clerics, at least in the concerns they offered publicly, the important points about coffee were the ways and intentions with which it was consumed, not the drink itself.[11] It was possible to drink even water incorrectly, for example, by passing a cup around as people did with wine—elsewhere, presumably, or out of sight. In the Muslim Middle East at the time coffee service began there, any practice of consuming a beverage that looked like ceremonial quaffing of wine was a violation of the spirit of Islam.

But the authorities' views changed. By 1574, the ulema across the region agreed that coffee should be legal.[12] The public demand for coffee and the revenue it produced for the state through taxes on coffeehouses and imported beans became too important to prohibit the drink. Coffee had become too popular to quash, and it suffered only temporary setbacks in the region: "The governments involved were unable to force on the populace edicts that proscribed the already [by the mid-1500s] deeply rooted habit of coffee drinking, and assemblies for that ostensible purpose."[13] Authorities continued to monitor conversations in coffeehouses, but as the talk did not lead to open sedition, let alone to resistance to established religious or secular authorities, concern about political and social issues subsided at the top levels of officialdom.

At the same time, Arab and Turkish commentators recognized and praised the mind-altering qualities of coffee. For example, Ibn Abd al-Ghaffar, writing in the late fifteenth or early sixteenth century, exclaimed, "It brings to the drinker a sprightliness of spirit and a sense of mental well-being."[14]

In the Arab world, attitudes toward coffee have shifted so much since the fifteenth century that "Arabic" coffee, made from powdery grounds and served in small cups, usually with cardamom added, is now considered a special token of hospitality and generosity. (In an effort to be politically and culturally correct, I call this kind of beverage Mediterranean coffee. Don't call it Turkish coffee in Greece, for instance.) "Arabic" coffee has become so symbolically important that it was "inscribed in 2015 . . . on the Representative List of the Intangible Cultural Heritage of Humanity" by UNESCO.[15]

As coffee reached England in the mid-seventeenth century, some of the same impact and disruption it had produced earlier in the Middle East appeared in the West. But the social and political effects went further in England, from helping to produce new views of gender to stirring the populace to innovative literary and political productions. Early English periodicals, first *The Coffee House Mercury* in the 1680s and several decades later *The Spectator* and *The Tatler*, emerged from coffee establishments.

The way that early English coffeehouses contributed to conversation had a positive influence, for a time, on views of women. The historian E. J. Clery

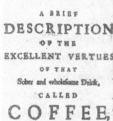

A BRIEF
DESCRIPTION
OF THE
EXCELLENT VERTUES
OF THAT
Sober and wholesome Drink,
CALLED
COFFEE,

AND ITS
INCOMPARABLE
EFFECTS
IN
PREVENTING or CURING
MOST
DISEASES
INCIDENT TO
HUMANE BODIES.

——*Florefcat Arabica Planta.*

WHen the sweet Poison of the Treacherous Grape,
  Had Acted on the world a General Rape;
  Drowning our very Reason and our Souls
In such deep Seas of large o'reflowing Bowls,
That New Philosophers Swore they could feel
The Earth to Stagger, as her Sons did Reel:
When Foggy Ale, leaving up mighty Trains
Of muddy Vapours, had besieg'd our Brains;
And Drink, Rebellion, and Religion too,
Made Men so Mad, they knew not what to do;
Then Heaven in Pity, to Effect our Cure,
And stop the Ragings of that Calenture,
First sent amongst us this *All-healing-Berry,*
At once to make us both *Sober* and *Merry.*
  Arabian Coffee, a Rich Cordial
To Purse and Person Beneficial,
Which of so many Vertues doth partake,
Its Country's called *Felix* for its sake.

'Tis stronger Drink, and base adulterate VVine,
Enfeebles Vigour, and makes Nature Pine;
Loaden with which, th' Impotent Sott is Led
Like a Sowc'd Hogshead to a Misses Bed;
But this Rare Settle-Brain prevents those Harms,
Conquers Old Sherry, and brisk Clarret Charms.
Sack, I defie thee with an open Throat,
VVhilst Truly COFFEE is my Antedote;
Methinks I hear Poets Repent th'have been,
So long Idolaters to that sparkling Queen;
For well they may perceive 'tis on Her score
APOLLO keeps them all so Cursed Poor;
Let them avoid Her tempting Charms, and then
VVe hope to see the VVits grow Aldermen;
In Breif, all you who Healths Rich Treasures Prize,
And Court not Ruby Noses, or blear'd Eyes,
But own Sobriety to be your Drift,
And Love at once good Company and Thrift;

Title page from the book A brief description of the excellent vertues of that Sober and wholesome Drink, called coffee, and its incomparable effects in preventing or curing most diseases incident to humane bodies. *The anonymous author contrasts the "sweet poison of the treacherous grape" to "coffee, a rich cordial beneficial to purse and person. . . . [It is for] all you who health's rich treasures prize."*
London: Printed for Paul Greenwood, 1674

writes that, "It was a bourgeois and paradoxically all-male institution, the coffee-house, that first generated discussion in England of women's role as a civilizing force" in the late seventeenth century. Earlier, the male ideal had been the "warrior-citizen."[16] Such males did not dirty their hands with commercial activities and regarded women as helpful ornaments and sexual vessels.

It is equally true that attractive women were often present behind coffeehouse bars, as decorative figures and targets for the lowest kind of humor. Nonetheless, the first issue of *The Tatler*, in 1709, appealed directly to "the Fair Sex."[17] As other possibilities for respectable masculine identity emerged, among them the businessman, old models of male warriors or statesmen began to weaken somewhat, which opened the way at least a little to admit other males as true men. Material status began to compete with birth and lineage to determine one's place in society, although that change dragged out in Britain for centuries and birth still has much resonance there. When more attention could be devoted to what one thought and wrote, exercising the mind, it became easier to believe that both male nonwarriors and women should be regarded as worthwhile people.

Leaving aside for the moment the question of whether the first English coffeehouses admitted women, Clery offers fascinating evidence from writings of the period that admired the high qualities of women's minds and moral behavior. One early periodical, the *Athenian Mercury*, invited women to contribute essays in 1691. The poet Elizabeth Rowe, who published often in the *Mercury* beginning in 1693, called herself a "coffee-house politician." These new claims and efforts by women had the effect, if only for a time, of undermining somewhat the warrior-citizen model in favor of a male who valued conversation, business, the world of ideas, and the moral and intellectual sense of women. Then, as the *Spectator* closed in 1713, Clery argues, the experiment in revaluing females also ended.[18] Men's clubs began to draw male customers of means away from coffeehouses and back into more private modes of interaction. Whether cause or effect of this change, the popular image of women again generally degraded them to the status of creatures merely available for men's use.

However subdued, supportive notes from voices by and about women remained important in English literature. A work that can make a claim to being the first novel in English, Samuel Richardson's *Pamela; or, Virtue Rewarded* (1740), owes much to the earlier discussions of feminine worth that characterized coffeehouse conversation and publications. Coffee is mentioned five times in the book. Richardson's novel *Clarissa, or, the History of a Young Lady*, which weighs in at one million words, is the story of a woman who struggles to keep her virginity against the advances of the evil Robert Lovelace. Clarissa loses, as Lovelace kidnaps and rapes her; she then refuses all food and drink and wastes away to a pure soul, on a much higher level than Lovelace. Clarissa is granted honorable feelings and moral superiority to the "gentleman" Lovelace.

Along with Richardson's literary admonitions about true virtue, especially as it related to interaction between men and women, the first English periodicals worked to promote proper behavior in men. This was especially important when merchants who were not members of the nobility began to emerge as a significant group, and interclass relations came to be much more than the nobility and gentry giving orders to lower beings.

Early British coffeehouses have also been identified as key sites for the rise of open political discussion and even for the appearance of political parties. In 1680, a pamphlet observed that the houses were filled with discussions "of religion and government. . . . All [patrons] are grown states-men,"[19] meaning that they discussed affairs of state. Such comments and the increasing number and popularity of coffeehouses in the late seventeenth century led the German scholar Jürgen Habermas to call what was happening the creation of a "bourgeois public sphere." By that phrase he meant a space where public discussion could go on, a venue for the "people's public use of their reason."[20] The coffeehouses were "bourgeois" because they were dominated by the middle classes, not the nobility. They were not private homes, the market square, or a church. Customers could talk, not just listen as at church. They could sit for hours drinking coffee and exchanging ideas and news.

Habermas's ideas have engendered much debate about the importance and popularity of coffeehouses. Yet his concept remains important for our understanding of how coffee helped shape a "widespread acceptance of the value of public opinion," as opposed to limiting discussion of politics and the formation of policy to a small number of well-born men. Furthermore, "there is little warrant for the claim that women were excluded from coffeehouses." They also took part in the new discussions.[21]

The intense interchange of news and ideas in the coffeehouses induced King Charles II of Britain, like Suleiman before him, to attempt to ban them in 1675. The monarch apparently feared that political life would spin further from his control, as the "states-men" and -women of the houses talked about national affairs. Charles also listened to the "high church royalists" who wanted to strengthen absolutist royal power as against the role of Parliament. Other leading figures in the campaign against coffeehouses wanted to promote good old English drinks—beer and ale—and the hearty life, for some, of hunting, gambling, and casual sex. Once more, the image of women suffered. Fun, not politics, could have been the motto of these "cavaliers."

Whatever the various motivations for Charles's edict were, his efforts failed, again replicating the earlier history of coffee in the Middle East. One reason is familiar: British coffeehouses brought considerable revenue to their owners and, in the form of licenses, to the government. But more important was an ironic point: Coffee had outgrown attempts to control it. A groundswell of opposition to overbearing royal authority, a new phenomenon that we might call public opinion, arose in the houses and in numerous pamphlets and petitions to the king. The coffeehouses had become powerful, at least so much so that shutting them down would have cost the Crown not only much effort and revenue, but also the loss of considerable popular support. Charles II, a would-be absolutist monarch, could not afford that outcome, given the fact that his own father had been deposed and executed during a rebellion and civil war in 1649.

Charles responded to protests about closing the coffeehouses with several extensions of their right to do business and with attempts to have royal spies report on patrons' conversations. Some proprietors were arrested, and a certain "climate of fear" descended on coffee drinkers.[22] But discussions and discontent with Charles II grew despite his grudging acquiescence to the desires of coffee lovers. English politics now ratcheted up to the Glorious Revolution of 1688, in which the new, avowed Catholic King James II, who had succeeded his brother Charles in 1685, was forced to yield to the Protestants William and Mary and to flee the country. As this happened, the question of what went on in the coffeehouses began to lose its importance, if haltingly and with numerous setbacks in the form of arrests and searches for seditious material.

By the first decades of the eighteenth century, and as the possibility of a Jacobite (referring to James and his descendants, i.e., Catholics) restoration faded, the English upper and middle classes accepted the central requirement of democracy: there could be multiple political parties that disagreed on various points but were all loyal to the basic structures and principles of government. Democracy is a rather delicate arrangement; in Britain, coffee was one of its main early lubricants.

The story of coffee's social impact across most of the European continent is quite different. First, Germany and Italy did not become united countries until the 1860s–1870s, so that much variation in reception and impact characterized those lands. By the mid-nineteenth century, coffeehouses were commonplace in the larger cities. Coffee did not arrive in Poland or Russia in any quantity, for example, until the early nineteenth century. However, coffee and its preparation received a prominent place in Poland's national epic poem, *Pan Tadeusz*, written by Adam Mickiewicz in 1834. Nor was there any particular chance for democracy or open discussion by commoners, whose influence was far less than in England, to take shape in most parts of the continent until the latter part of that century. Spain, meanwhile, adopted chocolate—as a drink—long before coffee made any real inroads there. Hot chocolate, perhaps because of its viscosity and intense sweetness, was never a "drink of reason"; instead, it was considered a mild aphrodisiac, probably based on the habits of the Aztec upper strata in drinking it before having sex.

Coffee took yet another path in France. In a way, the country's people were even more stratified than were England's. The First Estate was the clergy, whose upper ranks were drawn from established nobility. The Second Estate was comprised of the nobles, who with their relatives in the higher clergy dominated the country. These were not hard and fast legal and social categories, as the Crown ennobled many a bourgeois for services—or money—rendered. But influence on the monarch, whose power was limited in practice not by formal institutions but by tradition and the necessity to honor debts, came largely through personal contacts among the most highly placed subjects. No parliament existed in France until the Revolution. The *parlements*, regionally based, were more appeals courts for their districts than anything else, although they had the authority to issue certain decrees. In this situation, especially after Louis XIV (ruled 1643–1715) had created a magnet for nobles at his palace of Versailles by the 1680s, independent, public discussion was hardly encouraged. At Versailles, Louis could dictate fashion, yoke the nobility to spending large sums to keep up with the king's taste, and influence their marriages and affairs. As yet, little pressure existed to change the political structure of the country. "L'état, c'est moi"—I am the state, Louis could famously declare.

In the seventeenth century, it was natural that tastes in food and drink at the French court would set the tone for the whole country. One of the earliest reports of coffee in France dates from 1660 and centers on Jean-Baptiste Colbert, chief economic adviser to Louis XIV. A friend of his (naturally, another high official) brought an affection for coffee, along with utensils for its preparation, back from a visit to Italy. Colbert then offered the drink to another key figure at court, Cardinal Jules Mazarin, who served as chief minister to both Louis XIII and Louis XIV. Mazarin loved the new beverage, although he hardly had time to enjoy it; he died in 1661.[23]

Jean de Thévenot published *Relation d'un voyage fait au Levant* (Relation of a voyage made to the Levant) in 1664, in which he described coffee in Istanbul as bitter and black, yet good for the stomach. "There is no one rich or poor who drinks less than two or three cups a day and which a husband is required to furnish to his wife."[24] Thévenot provided an engraving of himself in Turkish dress as the frontispiece to the book, personally endorsing the exotic East and its habits.

The growing popularity of coffee in France is evident in a declaration by Louis XIV in 1692 that the state would have a monopoly on its sale, in the name of increasing royal revenue. And since it was France, the king immediately granted the privilege of trading in coffee to a "farmer," in this sense a person who would pay up front for the right to operate a monopoly or to collect taxes on specified items,[25] legally skimming off a significant portion. French monarchs were forever desperate for funds in the short run; to get quick cash, the government sold the rights to future revenue. By 1789, along with a few other major problems, this practice put the state into such a deep financial hole that it could not survive.

Despite Louis's decree, coffeehouses, or the ubiquitous word *café*, spread widely in France. In the decades left before the Revolution erupted, the monarchs themselves enjoyed coffee. Louis XV (who ruled from the age of five in 1715 until his death in 1774) loved the beverage. His chief mistress, Madame de Pompadour, had herself painted in "Oriental" dress by Carle van Loo in 1747 as *Sultane*, usually translated as Turkish Lady. She is accepting a cup of coffee handed to her by a black slave, a figure that also represented, in person or in art, the exotic lure of the East. The Revolution aimed at first to level the social distinction and luxury of the aristocracy depicted in the painting, to accord with the slogan "liberty, equality, and fraternity."

The ad indicates that the lure of the East had not disappeared from coffee promotions by the late nineteenth century. Indeed, many other illustrations used similar themes—for example, Rajah Coffee. Unfortunately, in the same period racist images of misshapen black people endorsing coffee and speaking in gibberish were also common.

In the meantime, the most noted *philosophe* of the eighteenth-century Enlightenment, Voltaire (1694–1778), frequented the cafes Procope and Régence, when he was allowed to live in Paris. At his home in exile in Ferney, Switzerland,

SULTANA

COFFEE

The **SULTANA COFFEE** is no vile, cheap mixture, but the blending of the very Choicest Naturally Ripened Coffees that are imported to this country. It is the result of over 20 years experience in the selecting, buying, roasting, blending, grinding and packing of Coffees It is packed the instant it is ground, in Perfectly Air-Tight Trade-Mark Caddies, holding exactly one and three pounds net—thus still retaining its Essential Oils, Great Strength, Delicious Flavor, and Rich Aroma, which are so absolutely necessary in a Perfect Coffee, and this is what we justly claim for the celebrated SULTANA COFFEE. Every Package Guaranteed as Represented, or it can be returned and the money refunded.

FOR SALE AT ALL OUR STORES.

120 STORES IN THE U. S.

The Great Atlantic and Pacific Tea Co.

Headquarters, 35 & 37 Vesey Street, N. Y.

N. B.—Owing to the great demand for our Celebrated SULTANA COFFEE, we are now packing it in ONE and THREE pound AIR-TIGHT TRADE-MARK CADDIES.

This ad, which dates from 1882, is an easily recognizable adaptation of a famous painting by Charles André (or Carle, Amédée, etc.) van Loo, done in 1747, of Madame de Pompadour, official mistress to King Louis XV of France. The Turkish figure in the background is not in the original painting.

With permission from the Warshaw Collection of Business Americana—Coffee, Archives Center, National Museum of American History, Smithsonian Institution he consumed copious quantities of coffee. His friends, alarmed by his habit, tried to persuade him to drink less. He replied, "I have been drinking coffee for more than fifty years; it is surely a poison, but up to the present, I have not felt any ill effects on my health."[26] In 1760, a comic play of his was translated into English as *The Coffee House, or Fair Fugitive*.

Although the Enlightenment thinkers are sometimes credited with producing the French Revolution—or, for that matter, with opening the road to Auschwitz—coffee consumption was socially contained in France, we might say, for decades before the fall of the Old Regime. Voltaire mocked certain nobles and spent time in exile and in the Bastille for his efforts, yet he and his fellow philosophes did not style themselves rebels. For the most part, they felt comfortable with the ruling elite, as demonstrated by Voltaire's extended stay with Frederick the Great of Prussia or by Denis Diderot's time with Catherine the Great of Russia. Back in France, it was not so much a bourgeois public sphere that influenced intellectual and political life in the eighteenth century as it was the private salon. Within the confines of a comfortable townhouse, women like Madame de Sévigné could host gatherings to hear the latest findings of scientists and the works of the philosophes—as long as they refrained from criticizing the elite, let alone the monarchy.

But underneath this more or less complacent surface, French publishers churned out many illegal volumes of new ideas unwelcome to the rulers. Other unprecedented influences traveled along the improved roads of the era,[27] and Englishmen did something to spread ideas as they wandered freely throughout the country. Eventually, France also saw its share of political discussions in coffeehouses, and on July 12, 1789, the radical Camille Desmoulins leaped onto a table in Paris outside the Café du Foy to incite a crowd against royal power. Two days later, the excitement carried over to the attack on the Bastille. The French Revolution, only a few days old, turned violent. Alas, democracy had a rough time emerging in France and endured setbacks as late as the Algerian War of the late 1950s to early 1960s. But none of that was coffee's fault.

Coffee played perhaps its final role in helping European political dissent to emerge shortly before the middle of the nineteenth century. Coffeehouses had become sites of discussion, especially in the separate parts of Germany, and of criticism by liberals of the conservative elite that ruled in many countries. Yet "1848 was the turning point at which modern history failed to turn," as the

British historian G. M. Trevelyan put it. Although barricades went up in streets from Paris to Frankfurt and Budapest, the "Revolutions of 1848" were defeated by conservative forces.

The last episode to date of coffee's connection to political upheaval took place in Latin America over the course of some one hundred years, from the late nineteenth to the late twentieth century. Coffee, as shown previously, reached the Caribbean in the 1720s and Brazil by the 1740s. But the crop lagged behind other agricultural products, especially leather and dyestuffs, into the mid-1800s. When coffee passed those items in value, it helped set in motion profound political change. Various "liberal" revolutions transformed the region, for instance, in El Salvador in 1885 and Nicaragua in 1893. In the Latin American setting of the day, "liberal" did not mean the promotion of progressive values for the down-trodden; on the contrary, it meant more freedom for a rising elite to make money and, usually, to exert more control and exploitation over the lower classes. Those strata comprised, above all, slaves and their descendants and indigenous peoples: Maya, Quechua, and many others.

The liberal revolutions of Latin America weakened or ended local people's rights to live autonomously on the land, reduced the Catholic Church's control of large amounts of property, and destroyed traditional monopolies and rights to tax locally produced goods and exports. Exactly none of that encouraged democracy. In short, Latin American liberalism in the nineteenth century was a successful movement to get government off the backs of a changing elite, now a mix of old aristocrats, a few rising families, and immigrants with money. All this was new freedom for a few. But with easier routes now open to land ownership and business, German, British, and Italian entrepreneurs arrived in a number of countries with the express purpose of growing coffee. They could see that Brazil was already doing well in exporting beans to the U.S. and Europe.

The newly arrived planters brought with them capital, financial expertise, and business skills that the old elite had never felt the need to master, living as it did on large estates that brought in enough money to buy fine clothes, horses, and luxury imports. To take a few examples, the Kühl and Vogel families settled in the area around Matagalpa, Nicaragua, in the 1880s, while J. Hill, a British adventurer, went to western El Salvador. Local Hispanic coffee-growing clans also did well for themselves; after the seizure of power in Costa Rica by General Tomas Guardia in 1870, the coffee elite ruled the country until 1948.[28] In

Nicaragua the Somoza and Chamorro families, with several others, dominated politics. Anastasio Somoza—of whom Franklin Roosevelt *may* have said, "He's a son of a bitch, but he's our son of a bitch"—who was also the son of a wealthy coffee planter, founded a dynasty in Nicaragua that ruled the country for more than forty years. Overthrown by the leftist Sandinistas after 1979, the old coffee elite in that country returned to power once more in the person of Violeta Chamorro, elected president in 1990, marking the first peaceful transition of office in Nicaragua in more than fifty years. She was able to bring peace to the country but not much else, as its economy continued to decline.

In Guatemala above all, but elsewhere in the region as well, indigenous peoples were long forced to work on coffee plantations at critical points during the year. Costa Rica avoided that fate and, in what was no accident, made exceptional progress toward democracy. That small country, which to this day has no army, moved forward to a much greater degree of social equality than nearby countries realized. That was partly because in Costa Rica, the indigenous people were all but wiped out early in colonization. In 2017, 83.6 percent of the population was counted as "white or mestizo." The second word means mixed, but in Costa Rica not necessarily dark-skinned. "Mulatto" people amounted to 6.7 percent of the inhabitants, and the indigenous citizens comprised only 2.4 percent. "Mulatto," derived from the Spanish for mule, is an old designation for people of mixed race. The term was used in U.S. census reports for many decades. In Costa Rica, "mulatto" refers to someone who cannot be called white or mestizo. Contrast all that with Nicaragua, just to the north, where the "white" population makes up 17 percent of the nation.[29] These differences in the two countries are quickly evident to anyone who has traveled there.

For Costa Rica, also dominated for many years at the national level by coffee growers, the absence of a large indigenous population produced a greater sense of unity among whites. By the same token, the racial difference that so often helped underpin social differences in Latin America did not exist in Costa Rica. Those factors in turn facilitated the growth of a respectable public school system by the late nineteenth century, a development that came only decades later, if at all, to the rest of the region. In the 1970s and '80s, when Central America was caught in a morass of civil war, interference by the U.S., and mass killings, Costa Rica remained calm and peaceful. It did not matter that the charismatic president, Oscar Arias Sanchez, was himself from an important coffee family. His grandfather had risen from poverty as an oxcart driver to become the country's largest single coffee exporter by 1935, but Arias had no ambition and no possibility of becoming a dictator.

In recent decades, the share of coffee in the value of exports has fallen in Latin America and in fact around the world. As recently as 1996–2000, fifteen countries earned more than 10 percent of their total export value through coffee. Today only seven nations fall into that category. Where coffee once dominated export earnings in Latin America, Costa Rica now earns only 3 percent of foreign income via coffee; Nicaragua holds the high mark for the region at 17 percent, while Colombia gets 7 percent in this way. In contrast, Burundi's figure is 59 percent of foreign earnings, Ethiopia's 33 percent.[30] Coffee will never again play the key and too often pernicious role in Latin American politics that it did for many decades, which is probably a very good thing. But coffee drinkers should remember that coffee trees have often been watered with blood as well as rain.

Coffee as an ingredient in social and political upheavals seems to have had its day. It may also have passed its peak as a drink of sociability. The office coffee pot and even the coffee break seem to have disappeared, in favor of single-serve pods and the isolation that earbuds provide. If I want to talk to customers in my own store once they have sat down, I often have to gesture first to get them to remove the headphones. Ever since Sony introduced the Walkman in 1979, people the world over have listened less and less to each other and more and more to canned sounds.

In my store, I have seen many planned meetings, some regular customers who have begun to sit and talk once in a while with other regulars, and many attempts by males to hit on the female baristas. We accommodate a regular group of retired men whom I think of as the philosophers; they meet almost every weekday morning to talk about books, poetry, cars, and whatever else comes to their minds.

But as a place to start conversations with strangers, let alone relationships with them? I think that's rare in any coffeehouse. Imagine going into a coffeehouse in Manhattan and trying to strike up a conversation with a person who happens to be sitting near you. Bryant Simon did strenuous research on sociability by sitting for many hours in Starbucks across the U.S.; he found that few conversations began among strangers.[31] Patrons may well go to coffeehouses to "be around other people, without actually having anything to do with them."[32]

No city in Eastern Europe has been more conquered by coffee in recent years than Prague. Of course, the city had many coffee traditions to draw from as the second city, behind Vienna, of the old Austro-Hungarian Empire.
Photo by Robert Thurston

Don't curb your enthusiasm quite so fast, however: coffeehouses are still often wonderful sites to listen to music, hear would-be poets at open mike sessions, and gather for coffee tastings. All of these are social functions to which coffee can still make an excellent contribution. And a coffeehouse just might be a fine place to meet a blind date; after all, it's just a cup of coffee.

COFFEE AND PERSONAL HEALTH

Almost from the first known records of coffee consumption, and for centuries after, doctors and public health officials disagreed about the drink's effects on the human body. The American advertising industry, during its most vibrant period, the 1880s into the 1970s, made wild claims for and against coffee's salubrity. Did coffee dry people out? Did it harm their sex lives, or perhaps improve them?

The first known advertisement for coffee, a broadsheet posted in London in 1652, claimed that coffee is "very good to help digestion." It was good for "sore

Eys" and headaches.[33] But in 1674 the infamous "Women's Petition against Coffee" ranted against the drink's supposed effect of "Drying up the Radical Moisture." Men never did wear *"greater Breeches,* or carry *less* in them of any *Mettle* whatsoever," with much more about how men were not able to hold up their end of things sexually.[34] But we have no idea who wrote the Petition or exactly what its aim was.

The debate went back and forth in the seventeenth century, with French doctors in particular weighing in for and against coffee's impact on health. Never were the judgments well founded in research or free from promotional inducements for or against coffee. Often, the opinions of "experts" versus coffee involved promotion of other drinks. For the most part, the debate died down when coffee usage became more widespread. The drink didn't seem to cause much harm, although it continued to be blamed for certain problems, especially heart trouble.

As coffee became more affordable and widely used, most physicians accepted the notion that in moderate quantities it was not harmful. Then a new round of the debate erupted in the 1890s. In the early years of the great, raucous era of American advertising, copy writers and business people lined up for and against the claims of Dr. John Harvey Kellogg. He insisted that coffee and tea were abominable beverages that played a major role in causing various nervous diseases. The dominant "race" in America, to use the terminology of the day, the Anglo-Saxons, now regularly expressed anxiety about their own hardiness and ability to reproduce in the face of the "New Immigration" from Italy and Eastern Europe. Would the old white stock of the country lose out to the reproductive capacity of the newcomers? Would the Anglo-Saxons simply be too nervous—the great disease they fought in this period was "neurasthenia," general nervous prostration—to be healthy or to reproduce? Dr. Kellogg, who ran an expensive residential clinic in Battle Creek, Michigan, became famous across the country as a health guru. Although he married, Kellogg and his wife believed in abstinence and maintained separate bedrooms; true, this was not helpful in the reproduction derby, yet Kellogg offered numerous appealing ideas, for that time, about how to improve one's health. Kellogg also shared an attitude common in the nineteenth and early twentieth centuries, that masturbation was harmful to the body; the practice could be deterred by eating bland foods, and certainly not meat.

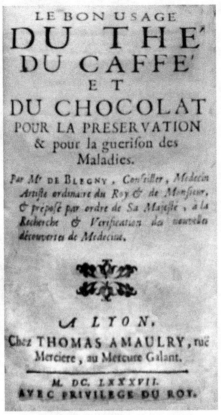

LE BON USAGE
DU THE'
DU CAFFE'
ET
DU CHOCOLAT
POUR LA PRESERVATION
& pour la guerison des
Maladies.

Par Mr DE BLEGNY, *Conseiller, Médecin
Artiste ordinaire du Roy & de Monsieur,
& preposé par ordre de Sa Majesté, à la
Recherche & Verification des nouvelles
découvertes de Médecine.*

A LYON,
Chez THOMAS AMAULRY, ruë
Merciere, au Mercure Galant.

M. DC. LXXXVII.
AVEC PRIVILEGE DU ROY.

Like the book A brief description of the excellent vertues . . . of coffee, *this French
tome celebrated the drink, while emphasizing tea and adding chocolate—as a hot
drink—to the mix. Coffee, tea, and chocolate arrived in Western Europe almost simultaneously in the mid-seventeenth century. Nicholas de Blegny published his contribution in 1687 in Lyon, France,* avec privilege du roy *("with the permission of the king").
The title may be translated as "Good Usage of tea, of coffee, and of chocolate, for
the preservation and cure of illnesses." De Blegny identified himself on the cover as a
"councilor, physician, and ordinary artist to the king." The campaign for coffee became
an important part of French medical discourse. However, there were some dissenting
French voices in the same period that claimed the drink was harmful—that it dried
people up and so on.*

The doctor's brother, Will Keith Kellogg, invented modern grain cereals, a
healthy alternative to eating eggs and meat each and every morning. The *Titanic*
featured John Harvey's exercise equipment, not all of it wacky, in its one and
only voyage. But with no serious investigations behind his ideas, the doctor

Colonic Machine

These devices were widely
used at the San. to treat
"toxicity" and constipation
brought on by the typical
diet & lifestyle of the day.

An enema machine, one of the more bizarre devices that Dr. Harvey Kellogg used on his pa-
tients. Far from all that he did was quackery; some of his machines, for example, one for rowing,
did provide serious exercise. Kellogg was also accounted a talented surgeon.
Kellogg Museum, Battle Creek, Michigan. Photo by Robert Thurston

insisted that certain kinds of exercise, a vegetarian diet, running electric current through the body, and several daily enemas, including one of yogurt, were essential for good health. In place of coffee, his preferred beverage was "Caramel Coffee," a grain product.[35] Food fads are not new.

But it was the Kelloggs' great rival in the breakfast business, C. W. Post, who really led the attack on coffee. Starting around 1907, he marketed Postum, another grain beverage. Switching from coffee to Postum would defeat the satanic "Mr. Coffee Nerves," who appeared in Postum ads into the 1930s. As a housewife harangues her bedraggled husband, the specter of Mr. Coffee Nerves lurks in the background. He whispers to the woman, "You're miserable, so keep it up. ... Make him miserable, too. Heh, heh, heh!"[36]

Reflecting the long-standing ambivalence about coffee, Chase and Sanborn ads announced in the same era that, "You'll do it better" with their products. This campaign featured beautiful young women in provocative poses next to well-muscled men. Needless to say, all the characters in these ads were white. The secret to greater satisfaction lay in drinking the company's "dated coffee," which was never stale.

Coffee could even prevent suicide, one helpful pamphlet announced in a cartoon and story at the beginning of the twentieth century. In recent years, the debate on coffee and health, fanciful or based however loosely on science, has all but ended, although claims for coffee's miraculous role in boosting happiness are still around.

What, in the light of substantial research published in the last few years, *does* happen to us when we drink coffee? The recent news is almost entirely in favor of the drink. An article titled "The Good Things in Life: Coffee as a Part of a Healthy Diet and Lifestyle," reported results of a survey carried out in 2015 of 4,119 respondents across ten European countries. Drawing on that study, Professor Chris Seal of Newcastle University, UK, wrote, "The facts about coffee are: coffee can be consumed as part of a healthy diet, and current scientific research suggests that moderate consumption of 3–5 cups of coffee a day can reduce the risk of some common, serious health conditions, including type 2 diabetes, cardiovascular disease, and cognitive decline."[37] Numerous other investigations cited in "The Good Things in Life" show the same results.

But perhaps research reported by something named the Institute for Scientific Research on Coffee is biased in the drink's favor. That certainly cannot

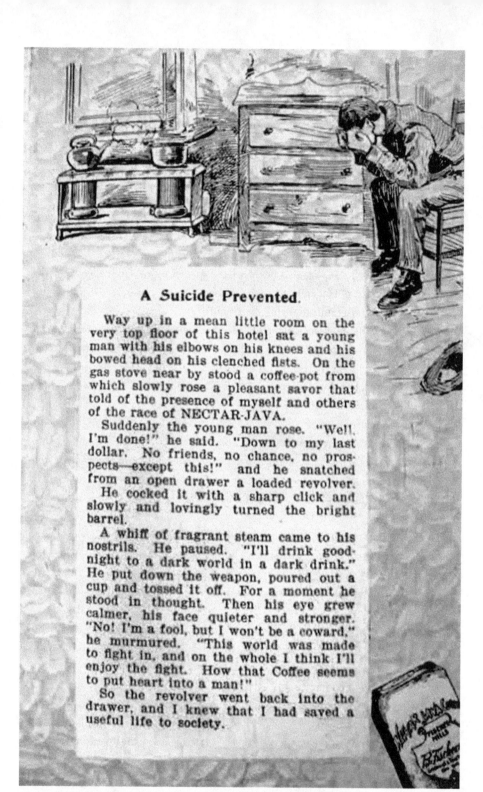

A Suicide Prevented.

Way up in a mean little room on the very top floor of this hotel sat a young man with his elbows on his knees and his bowed head on his clenched fists. On the gas stove near by stood a coffee-pot from which slowly rose a pleasant savor that told of the presence of myself and others of the race of NECTAR-JAVA.

Suddenly the young man rose. "Well, I'm done!" he said. "Down to my last dollar. No friends, no chance, no prospects—except this!" and he snatched from an open drawer a loaded revolver.

He cocked it with a sharp click and slowly and lovingly turned the bright barrel.

A whiff of fragrant steam came to his nostrils. He paused. "I'll drink goodnight to a dark world in a dark drink." He put down the weapon, poured out a cup and tossed it off. For a moment he stood in thought. Then his eye grew calmer, his face quieter and stronger. "No! I'm a fool, but I won't be a coward," he murmured. "This world was made to fight in, and on the whole I think I'll enjoy the fight. How that Coffee seems to put heart into a man!"

So the revolver went back into the drawer, and I knew that I had saved a useful life to society.

Maybe coffee has long been a miracle drink.

From Life and Adventures of a Coffee Bean as Told by Himself. New York: B. Fischer Company, 1901 be said of the most prestigious medical journal in the U.S., the *New England Journal of Medicine* (*NEJM*). In 2012, it reported on a massive survey of more than 400,000 men and women who drank coffee. The survey followed an even larger group, asking about their dietary habits and exercise from 1995–1996 until completion of the investigation in 2008. When people who smoked or already had cancer or heart disease—factors not taken into account in many previous surveys—were removed from the results, clear benefits from drinking coffee emerged. This was so despite that fact that

> as compared with persons who did not drink coffee, coffee drinkers were more likely to smoke cigarettes and consume more than three alcoholic drinks per day, and they consumed more red meat. Coffee drinkers also tended to have a lower level of education; were less likely to engage in vigorous physical activity; and reported lower levels of consumption of fruits, vegetables, and white meat.[38]

Who knew that coffee drinkers were bums? At least they were smart enough to drink the stuff. When compared with men who did not drink coffee, men who consumed six or more cups of coffee per day had a 10 percent lower risk of death during the span of the study, whereas women in this category of consumption had a 15 percent lower risk. The best results were among women who drank four to five cups a day; they died at a rate 16 percent less over the course of the whole study than women who did not drink coffee. Remarkably, "Similar associations were observed whether participants drank predominantly caffeinated or decaffeinated coffee." Obviously that pushes us to wonder what else in coffee is good or bad for you. With 800–1,000 volatile organic compounds to examine, it will be some time before researchers can answer that question definitively.

The *NEJM* article noted that,

> In summary, this large prospective cohort study showed significant inverse associations of coffee consumption with deaths from all causes and specifically with deaths due to heart disease, respiratory disease, stroke, injuries and accidents, diabetes, and infections. Our results provide reassurance with respect to the concern that coffee drinking might adversely affect health.[39]

Just to be clear, "inverse associations" means less risk from the listed problems than was the case among non–coffee drinkers.

The Harvard School of Public Health has been more cautious. Still, a Harvard study of more than 130,000 volunteers over an 18–24-year period found no detrimental effects on health from drinking coffee—unless you are drinking so much that it causes tremors! More forcefully, as Dr. Rob van Dam of the Harvard School wrote in 2015,

> Research over the past few years suggests that coffee consumption may protect against type 2 diabetes, Parkinson's disease, liver cancer, and liver cirrhosis. And our latest study on coffee and mortality found that people who regularly drank coffee actually had a somewhat lower risk of death from cardiovascular disease than those who rarely drank coffee; this result needs to be confirmed in further studies, however.[40]

Van Dam did not mention the *NEJM* article. Besides the fact that more research is always indicated, the Harvard study goes well beyond the finding of no detrimental effects from drinking coffee.

A survey of the scientific literature on coffee health up to 2011 concluded that, "All these lines of actions adopted by coffee or caffeine [in the body] eventually help in controlling the path leading to Parkinsonism." The authors went on to conclude that, "Intake of 2–3 cups/daily of coffee can improve cognitive functioning, the sense of sensation [i.e., heightens sensations], as well as digestion. Moreover, the same dosage could be effective against coronary heart diseases, diabetes mellitus, cancer lines, Parkinsonism, and Alzheimer's disease."[41]

The *Tufts University Health and Nutrition Letter* for April 2016 summarized an article on "Effects of Habitual Coffee Consumption on Cardiometabolic Disease, Cardiovascular Health, and All Cause Mortality," published in the prestigious *Journal of the American Heart Association*.[42] The Tufts *Letter* quoted Alice H. Lichtenstein, DSc, director of Tufts' HNRCA Cardiovascular Nutrition Laboratory: "These findings mean that if you enjoy coffee or tea, you can continue to do so without any concern about your heart." Another old idea about coffee must be discarded.

Lichtenstein served as vice chair of the 2015 Dietary Guidelines Advisory Committee, which concluded that drinking three to five cups of coffee a day (up to about 400 milligrams of caffeine) was safe and might even be associated with lower risk of type 2 diabetes and cardiovascular disease. Lichtenstein noted that, "It is important to remember the caveat that we are talking about coffee and tea, not the cream and sugar that may be added to it. Those can contribute un-needed calories, in the form of added sugar and saturated fat."

Caffeine consumption in coffee, several recent studies show, can not only help reduce the risk of getting Parkinson's disease, it can improve the condition of people who already have it.[43] It would seem that, except for the groups already noted—people with especially high blood pressure and so forth—there is rarely a reason to stop drinking coffee.

Perhaps it's going a bit far to say that, "Higher coffee consumption is associated with a lower risk of death, according to research presented today at ESC [European Society of Cardiology] Congress" (August 17, 2017). My risk of death, like yours, dear reader, is 100 percent. That doesn't change if each day I drink five cups of coffee, five bottles of gin, or five cans of kerosene. Fortunately, the report goes on to specify that 19,896 participants were followed over a ten-year period. In that span, those subjects who consumed "at least four cups of coffee per day had a 64% lower risk of all-cause mortality than those who never or almost never consumed coffee." That, of course, is a much stronger figure than the *NEJM* reported. And in the European study, "there was a 22% lower risk of all-cause mortality for each two additional cups of coffee per day." Perhaps most striking in these results is a new finding, that among participants at least "45 years old, drinking two additional cups of coffee per day was associated with a 30% lower risk of mortality during follow-up."[44] Perhaps the European subjects of the ESC study drank less alcohol and exercised more than the participants in the *NEJM* survey? Or had more olive oil and fish in their diets? We should watch for even more finely tuned investigations of coffee and diet.

Imagine for a moment what four to five cups of coffee per day could do for someone who doesn't smoke, doesn't drink much alcohol or eat much red meat, and who gets off the couch to exercise regularly. Such a person would have an excellent chance, all other things being equal, of staying healthy and alive for quite a long time. What more motivation could anyone ask for drinking coffee?

CAFFEINE

A closer look at caffeine, the world's most popular psychoactive chemical, is in order. "Psychoactive" means simply "a substance that affects the mind," in

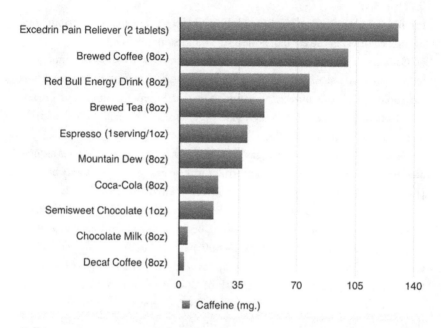

Caffeine content in various drinks and medicines.
Sources: Center for Science in the Public Interest, Mayo Clinic, *The Guardian*, *Healthline Newsletter*, Cleveland Clinic. Chart by Lara Thurston

this case, yes, making it more active. Coffee is a mild upper, a central nervous system stimulant. That characteristic is one reason that people used to pair it so frequently with cigarettes, which are mild downers. Think of all the songs about coffee and reefer, to take a different substance. Tea and reefer? That sounds odd, although tea also contains caffeine, as do energy drinks, many soft drinks, headache medicines, and kola nuts, among other plants and products.

Caffeine was first isolated from coffee in 1819. That discovery happened because the great German writer Johann Wolfgang von Goethe, who was fascinated by chemistry, heard about the work of a young chemist, Friedlieb Runge, on various subjects. Specifically, Goethe wanted to see how Runge could make a cat's pupils dilate by dropping extract of belladonna into the poor animal's eyes. The two men set up a meeting, and on the appointed day, legend has it, Runge donned formal wear and walked across the campus of the University of Berlin, holding his cat under one arm. Runge was not especially popular with students; watching him proceed in such stately dress, holding a cat, they called out, "Hier kommt Doktor Gift!" (Here comes Dr. Poison!). But the jokes ended when Runge explained that he was going to meet Germany's most celebrated writer.

Goethe, if not the cat, was impressed by the dilation demonstration. Shortly after, he asked Runge to take on the challenge of isolating the active chemicals in coffee. Within several months, Runge finished the task. He called the most active ingredient *Kaffeebase*, coffee base, that is, a compound with pH above seven. The word *caffeine* (German *Koffein*) appeared first in French, as *caféine*, in 1822.

Apparently neither Runge, Goethe, nor anyone else at the time seriously investigated the physiological or psychoactive effects of caffeine. The beginnings of methodical inquiry into that subject had to wait until scientists knew more precisely what caffeine was. French chemists worked on the problem for decades, but it was another German who achieved success. In 1895–1897, Hermann Emil Fischer synthesized caffeine and discovered its chemical structure. It turns out that caffeine is indeed an alkaloid base, which scientists put in the methylxanthine class. *Methyl* means hydrogen bonded to carbon, while xanthine is produced in many animals and plants, quite naturally. Xanthines derived from plants or produced synthetically may be used to treat asthma and airway blockage in people, although drugs of this class are not the first choice for such relief.

Caffeine probably developed in some plants as a defense mechanism; few animals, as we know, eat coffee fruit. In the human body, caffeine increases heart rate, elevates blood pressure somewhat, and typically sharpens the intellect for a while. That is, chess players, pilots, and athletes, to name a few active types, do better after drinking caffeine-laden beverages. The scientific consensus regarding basic cognitive functions is that caffeine "in doses from 32 to 300 mg" for a 75-kilogram individual (165 pounds) "enhances fundamental aspects of cognitive performance, such as attention, vigilance, and reaction time." Scientists generally agree that "caffeine improves 'lower' cognitive functions such as simple reaction time, whereas caffeine's effects on 'higher' cognitive functions such as problem solving and decision making are often debated." But the disagreements continue partly because there are not many studies of "higher" brain functions and caffeine. Coffee increases vigilance, and it certainly helps alertness during long and largely boring activities like sentry duty and highway driving. If you fly a U-2 spy plane (there are still some working out there), you will be glad to know that in simulations of overnight flights, coffee helped keep up pilots' attention.[45]

Athletes are keenly aware of what caffeine can do for them. American college athletes, under the rules of the National Collegiate Athletic Association, are limited to a caffeine concentration in the urine of 15 mcg/ml. That means no more than 15 micrograms of caffeine per milliliter of urine, or, to give a very rough average, about 800 milligrams of caffeine in the body. Caffeine is quickly diluted in humans, hence the much lower amount of caffeine in urine. If we assume that the average 12-ounce cup of coffee—although no such thing as an "average" amount of caffeine exists, as I will show—has about 100 milligrams of caffeine, it would take eight cups downed in a fairly short time, no more than a few hours, to put an "average" athlete over the allowed limit,[46] although the NCAA speaks of 500 milligrams in the body. Eight cups or 96 ounces (about 2.84 liters, or nearly 3 U.S. quarts) is one heck of a lot of coffee to drink, even over the span of several hours. This is something else not to try at home or before you play in a big game. Besides, you would probably have to urinate often, and there are only so many time-outs.

Caffeine is readily absorbed in the body, reaching its peak level within an hour in most people; if taken with or just after eating, absorption will be slower. Coffee can interfere with sleep because of the caffeine in it. That happens because caffeine is close in structure to adenosine, a compound that the body manufactures as you get drowsy. Caffeine is one of a relatively few substances people ingest that easily crosses the blood-brain barrier (BBB), because it is both water soluble and fat soluble. The BBB is a semi-permeable membrane—a thin layer of tissue that allows some chemicals to pass through while blocking others—surrounding the brain. It is "an important mechanism for protecting the brain from fluctuations in plasma composition, and from circulating agents such as neurotransmitters and xenobiotics"[47] (the last word refers to foreign substances not produced by the organism itself—drugs, poisons, and so on).

The BBB generally blocks chemicals capable of disturbing neural function. Caffeine passes through the barrier and quickly fits into adenosine receptors in the brain, preventing them from taking up adenosine. However, caffeine doesn't fit perfectly into the receptors, which leaves a kind of gap that prevents the intruder from cuing all of adenosine's functions.[48] Those include partly shutting down the production of other chemicals in the body. Some "of the brain's own natural stimulants (such as dopamine) work more effectively when the adenosine receptors are blocked, and all the surplus adenosine floating around in the brain cues the adrenal glands to secrete adrenaline, another stimulant."[49]

Yet if caffeine regularly enters the brain, that organ will react by creating more adenosine receptors. The effects of caffeine will be in effect managed better, and the body will settle into a routine—most of the time—that allows sleep and shuts down the extra production of adrenaline.

Adenosine receptors are found on "virtually every cell in the body."[50] Since they are found in the kidneys, when the receptors are blocked by caffeine the blood vessels there dilate, which results in increasing "the filtration rate and producing more urine. . . . Caffeine is also a laxative [which] . . . in the colon causes a *constriction*," quite different from the effect in the kidneys. The result in the bowels for a distinct minority of drinkers may be an increased, even urgent need to defecate.[51]

When caffeine wears off, that is, when it is metabolized and passed from the body in urine, adenosine can do its job. How long does caffeine stay in the body? Perhaps five to six hours before it is metabolized enough to end its effects and for it to begin to pass from the body. That process depends on your singular chemical makeup. Caffeine's half-life in smokers may be only some three hours, while women taking oral contraceptives may experience twice the average time. Babies can actually process caffeine as fast at the age of six months as adults can.[52] But in general caffeine's half-life in the body is shortest in males of European descent, longest in pregnant Asian women. So many things not to try at home!

Caffeine is in many headache remedies because it blocks adenosine, whose levels go up sharply during migraines. Caffeine "antagonizes adenosine receptors," causing "cerebral vasoconstriction."[53] That's why blood pressure goes up. Think of forcing water through a hose large in diameter, then forcing the same flow of water through a smaller hose. To get through the second hose, the pressure of the water has to go up. As caffeine works on blood vessels in the head, and given that it gets into the brain pretty quickly, it makes vessels there constrict and shrink away a bit from softer brain tissue. It is the pressure of the blood vessels on that softer tissue and vice versa that make the head ache in the first place.

I once had an overnight guest in my house who had a terrible headache. He had taken several headache pills, but they didn't help. I tried massaging his scalp and

neck, to no avail. Finally I said, "Drink some coffee. It may help." He replied, "But then I won't go to sleep." I answered, "I think it's better to go without some sleep than to suffer serious pain, which may well keep you awake anyway." So he drank two cups of coffee that I made for him. He started to feel better, and after several hours he was able to go to sleep. If you have that kind of tough choice to make, I can only say, "Use your head."

The action of caffeine on blood vessels in the brain also helps explain why some people get headaches if they withdraw from coffee, or even if they miss a cup in the morning. The brain is used to the pushback that caffeine provides to its circulatory system, and other tissue can bear down on blood vessels more easily. Moreover, since the brain may have produced additional adenosine receptors and has adjusted to their presence and to the chemical and physical changes that can produce, the body now has to operate with a kind of overload in some respects. That too can make your head hurt.

If you are really trying to kick a coffee habit, and you can hold out for seven to twelve days without a cup, the brain should readjust and get back to normal.[54] But all this raises the question of why, unless you are stuck on the proverbial desert island, you would want to do without the pleasure and stimulation that coffee provides.

How much caffeine does any cup of coffee contain, and how much is bad for you? The second question is a little easier to answer, at least in a crude form. For most people, a lethal dose of caffeine would be around 10 grams, or what you might get from drinking a hundred of those "average" cups in the span of a few hours. But your body would probably rebel long before you drank that much coffee; either you just couldn't take any more or you would vomit, removing some of the offending liquid before it got into your blood.

The question of how much caffeine is in any drink is vexed. The easy part of this issue is that tea—to make a gross generalization—has about 40 percent of the amount of caffeine that coffee does in the same size drink. Espresso may also have around that same figure compared to brewed coffee, but of course espresso is much more concentrated. To measure the amount of caffeine accurately in a beverage, you would have to drag a gas chromatograph around with you. Since those tend to cost upward of $8,000 and are heavy and bulky, that idea probably won't work.

The Mayo Clinic, among numerous other institutions, has investigated the amount of caffeine in coffee drinks. Mayo indicates that in 8 ounces (237 milliliters) of brewed coffee the number of milligrams of caffeine typically ranges from 95 to 165. The same size of brewed decaf will have only 2–5 milligrams of caffeine. A typical shot of espresso at 1 ounce (30 milliliters) has 47–64 milligrams of caffeine. Eight ounces of brewed black tea contains between 28 and 45 milligrams of caffeine.[55] So not only does Mayo find that caffeine content varies over a substantial range—for brewed coffee, the high figure of 165 milligrams is almost 74 percent greater than the low number, 95—but the clinic's range is higher than most earlier studies showed.

Some caffeine may still be present in decaf coffee. A study published in 2006 found that the amount from ten coffee shops in Florida varied from 0 to 13.9 milligrams in 16-ounce servings.[56] In the U.S., federal law as administered by the Department of Agriculture stipulates that a reduction in caffeine by "97.5% is the legally accepted method of calculation."[57] So how much caffeine is left depends on how much was in the beans to start with. For the vast majority of people who physiologically need to drink decaf, there is probably nothing to worry about in these ranges. But it's good to be aware of the issue if caffeine affects you strongly.

It is difficult to say which varieties of coffee will produce more caffeine in the cup. One study indicates that, on the high side, "'Catuai' has some 1.34 percent caffeine in the green beans, while 'Laurina' has .62 percent. But 'Laurina' is a rare plant, partly because it is highly susceptible to leaf rust. In arabica beans, caffeine content averages 1.2% while robusta figures at 2.2%."[58] Since cross-breeding continues at a rapid pace, the question of how much caffeine is in a cup of arabica is a moving target. My own feeling is that, unless you are especially sensitive to caffeine, the differences among arabica varieties are not worth worrying about.

Dark roast coffee may have slightly less caffeine than light roasts, as explained earlier, but the amount is not usually significant. In any event, the important factor is not how much is in a single cup, but how much is ingested overall.

RECENT RESEARCH ON COFFEE AND HEALTH

Coffee, more precisely caffeine, is addictive, or so many people and studies say. The *Oxford English Dictionary* defines addiction as "immoderate or compulsive consumption of a drug or other substance; spec[ifically] a condition characterized by regular or poorly controlled use of a psychoactive substance despite adverse physical, psychological, or social consequences, often with the development of physiological tolerance and withdrawal symptoms."[59] That sounds pretty bad, and coffee does fit this description *for the most part*, although it is hardly heroin. Yet does coffee produce "adverse consequences"? No, not by itself; when was the last time you heard of a coffee fiend robbing people to feed an addiction? People sitting quietly in a coffeehouse, talking to each other or sticking to themselves, would not today seem to represent or cause negative "social consequences." We are not in Mecca in 1511 or London in 1675.

The next important compounds present in a cup of unfiltered coffee—espresso or French press, for example—are diterpenes, oily substances. The two diterpenes in coffee liquor are cafestol and kahweol, names obviously derived from studies of coffee. Filters, especially paper ones, trap these two chemicals, while unfiltered liquor—again, espresso or from a French press—retains them.

It may be good or bad to have diterpenes in your brew. They may raise your cholesterol level. If that is a concern, drink filtered liquor. On the other hand, there are indications that cafestol and kahweol "could have some anticancer effects and be good for the liver."[60]

Antioxidants are present in coffee. They help prevent cancer, as they "sop up reactive molecules before they have a chance to harm sensitive tissue like the lining of blood vessels."[61] A specific study of antioxidants in coffee made with paper filters concluded that "coffee consumption prevents endogenous [internal to the body] formation of oxidative DNA-damage in humans."[62] Coffee appears to reduce the risk of skin cancer, specifically malignant melanoma, as shown in a study of 447,357 retirees over ten years. Those respondents who drank four or more cups of coffee a day were 20 percent less likely to develop the disease.[63] Obviously, staying out of the sun and wearing sunscreen while in it are the best protections, yet coffee appears to score another point in this case. The reduced risk of other cancers among coffee drinkers has been noted above. Yet another important finding is that, "Compared with no coffee consumption, every additional cup of coffee consumed per week was associated with a 7% decrease in the risk of HF [heart failure] and an 8% decrease in the risk of stroke."[64] Go and get a cup of coffee now!

There is one recently identified, problematic issue associated with coffee—in this instance, with roasting—acrylamide. Probably this natural compound has always existed in some cooked food, but it was not found there until 2002.[65] Acrylamide develops from low concentrations of the amino acid asparagine and free sugars. Acrylamide is a by-product of the Maillard browning reactions that occur during roasting or frying at high temperatures, but not from boiling or steaming. Its presence relates to surface area of the cooked product, so that much more of it occurs in potato chips than in coffee. Darker roasts have less acrylamide than lighter ones, and the time of a roast is most important in producing it, not the ultimate temperature reached.

Is acrylamide in coffee a problem? According to former National Coffee Association President Robert Nelson, "The highest level of the compound occurs at a roasting level too light for consumer preferences, after which it begins to degrade significantly during further roasting. Completed roasting leaves only a fraction of the original acrylamide levels in the bean. Moreover, there's very little acrylamide left in brewed coffee as it is consumed."[66]

The compound has been shown to cause cancer in laboratory animals, but only when they are exposed to quantities, or have actually been made to eat acrylamide, at a level "1000–100,000 times larger than the usual amounts . . . humans are exposed to" through diet.[67] At present, "we consume less acrylamide [from all sources] than the maximum exposure levels recommended by the European Food Safety Authority."[68] Certainly much more research needs to be done; but "several epidemiological studies examining the relationship between dietary intake of acrylamide and cancers of the colon, rectum, kidney, bladder, and breast have been undertaken. These studies found no association between intake of specific foods containing acrylamide and risk of these cancers. Moreover, there was no relationship between estimated acrylamide intake in the diet and cancer risk."[69]

The U.S. Food and Drug Administration looked into acrylamide levels in grocery store foods; among coffees, instant had the highest concentrations.

But the compound levels are even worse in some frozen french fries and cereals. In drinking specialty coffee, it appears to be nothing to worry about, even though the state of California has put acrylamide on a list of 800 carcinogenic substances. Harmless or not, a Los Angeles court decision in March of 2018 will probably lead to required warning labels about acrylamide for coffee, however it is sold in California. Coffee shops may have to hang warning signs on their walls. All this, at least to people in the coffee industry, seems to be based on vastly exaggerated fears of poisons in our food.

Probably the biggest risk from acrylamide in coffee is for people who roast it, in rooms with relatively high concentrations of the substance.[70] That problem could be handled by improved ventilation around roasting equipment. Other ways of reducing acrylamide in coffee include trying to roast it with steam or treating it with bacterial enzymes. To say the least, these ideas have not caught on in a big way in the coffee industry.

Diacetyl is another problematic chemical that is present or produced by roasting coffee. Over time, it can damage the respiratory system and cause reduced lung function. The authors of a report from the Centers for Disease Control and Prevention recommend that roasteries should be "operating the exhaust fan and make-up air system in the production space whenever occupied; installing local exhaust ventilation; implementing administrative controls such as modification of work practices; and training employees about work-place hazards. We also recommend instituting a medical monitoring program."[71] Everyone in the coffee industry expects that the harmful effects of diacetyl can be avoided by these measures.

Despite the flap over acrylamide and the problem for roasters posed by diacetyl, the advice from recent studies on coffee and health continues to be overwhelmingly positive. Looking back to the *Harvard Health Letter* report on coffee of January 2012, somewhat dated now by even more encouraging findings but still of considerable value, the report card on coffee drinking is:

- Alzheimer's: "hints of protection."
- Cancer: lower risk for some types, for example, endometrial, but not for others, such as esophageal. (As we have seen, other findings go much farther in citing enhanced protection from cancer.)
- Diabetes: lower risk.

- Heart attack: can increase "some factors (homocysteine) associated with higher risk." But moderate consumption, 1–3 cups a day, "has been linked to a small decrease in risk," especially for women.
- Liver disease: lower risk, except that cafestol and kahweol (in unfiltered coffee, as noted above) "may be responsible for liver benefits."
- Parkinson's: "moderate (25%) decrease in risk." (Sounds like a serious decrease to me.)
- Stroke: intake of 3–4 cups a day "is associated with lower risk." However, "chance of a stroke may increase immediately after intake, particularly among infrequent consumers."[72]

The report concludes that, "All of the favorable studies and all of the seemingly healthful ingredients in coffee are good news for coffee drinkers. They can relax and enjoy their habit."

To that endorsement can be added the view of the Institute for Scientific Information on Coffee in 2017, that "Overall, a moderate consumption of coffee, equivalent to 3–5 cups per day, has been associated with a range of desirable physiological effects in scientific literature and can fit within a healthy, balanced diet and active lifestyle."[73]

So, drink up and feel good.

5

Conclusion

Looking back to the mountains of coffee country, it seems to me that hope outweighs despair. But perhaps not by much. The many programs designed to help farmers and workers, from women's health to better communications and training, touch millions of people every day, yet many coffee people never encounter these efforts.

For the moment, the world "benchmark" C price for coffee is not too bad, at $122.72 per 100 pounds on December 8, 2017, imported into New York and elsewhere. At that price, and given the numerous adjustments upward related to that price, many farmers can survive, at least in the short run. As we have seen, a host of factors, from a bumper crop in a large producing country to a drought or flood, make the price change. Since more growers are figuring out how to raise productivity and how to defend their crops against pests, I personally do not expect more than an occasional temporary upswing for midlevel arabica. Yet the new and improved facilities for processing that I have visited in several countries, proof that farmers' income is rising for high-quality beans, give me a sense of optimism about the future.

The same is true when I visit researchers who are putting their best efforts into confronting and containing coffee's many enemies. I admire the groups and individuals who work long hours, often not in the best conditions, to look more deeply into the genetics of the plant, the qualities of soil, and the effects of climate on coffee. In coffee's race against time, which so far helps both global warming and the spread of pests, the scientists have accomplished much and will make further advances in the future.

Researchers on health and coffee have done the world a mighty service in the past few years by assuring us that a beloved beverage is actually good for us. Some day, we will know exactly how, when, what kind, and how much coffee any individual should drink for maximum health benefits. Maybe then we can stay ahead of the robots.

The coffee shop entrepreneurs and fanatical roasters who dream up new techniques and then build the necessary equipment have my respect and admiration. If once in a while the talk and the styles of dress and hair aspire to more importance than the coffee itself has, part of that comes with reaching for the best possible product.

How can anyone who loves coffee help improve the earth, farmers' income, and health? The farmers naturally bear most of the worry and effort to save the environment, but they are being assisted with money and the results of research from many directions. I have yet to meet a coffee grower, or in fact anyone in the industry, who didn't care deeply about the earth. With all that's going on to protect coffee, it may actually survive what humans in general are doing to the planet.

I have tried to coin another new word, "gringoism." It means to "go down to X country and 'help,' with little or no understanding of what conditions are like down there." But in almost every case I've seen, coffee people from the North are good about not sticking their noses and advice in where they are not wanted. When pickers have their children along, there is probably a solid reason for bringing them. If people are sorting coffee cherries by hand, consider that otherwise they might have no income at all. It's not that we Northerners should always look on the bright side of coffee; far from it. Yet we should be aware that it is not our role to tell people on the ground what to do. To offer specific kinds of expertise and aid is fine, and to listen carefully is probably even better.

Roast Magazine recently asked several leading figures in the coffee industry for their opinions on "the most pressing concern in coffee today—and what they think we as specialty coffee professionals should be doing about it." Here is a summary of their answers and the issues they identified:

- Climate change: "We must work together over a long term."
- Value for farmers, as consumers demand both lower prices and higher quality: "[Give] coffee producers a fair shake."
- Sustainable supply: "Provide more knowledge to origin and to producers so that they can better understand their own product."
- Sustainability of the whole coffee chain: "[We need a joint] commitment of all supply chain stakeholders to guarantee sustainability."
- The need to double production by 2050 even as climate change endangers coffee farms: "[What is required is] professionalization of the coffee sector at origin with research, extension and education aimed at farmer profitability."[1]

This book has addressed these issues throughout. I would further emphasize one point: More money needs to go into farmers' hands, so consumers should look for coffee that costs more than the brown liquid at a gas station or fast-food restaurant. Seeking satisfaction beyond the large chains might also be helpful. Buy good-quality whole beans from a reputable roaster and grind them at home. Don't hesitate to ask your local supplier where the coffee comes from—which should be on every label—and whether the importer can truly say that the price paid to farmers benefits them. While it is nice to think that by buying a certified coffee, you are automatically helping producers, my view is that it is better still to think about the price you pay per pound, bearing in mind that a dollar goes much farther in Uganda, for example, than in Costa Rica or Hawaii. Buy quality coffee, but not the absurd poop coffee and other gimmicky beans, and let the farmers spend the money as they see fit. They often live in tightly knit communities where they help each other.

Coffee's past, present, and future are simultaneously bright and bleak. I prefer to think of the many positive aspects of the industry and about the hard-working, capable people I have met in fields, research stations, and shops. Coffee folks are almost always wonderfully generous with their time and knowledge. On more than a few trips, I've been passed from one person to another and not allowed to pay for time, meals, or coffee. All that has not been a question of business in the narrow sense, because I'm not a green coffee buyer. That's just the way coffee people are, once they find out you are committed to their product.

I hope that professionals of the coffee clan will get pleasure and some new information from this book. As for people who just enjoy the world's greatest beverage, and more broadly anyone interested in critical issues of social justice, agriculture, and globalization, I hope this brief introduction to a wonderfully complex subject will leave everyone wanting more, and better, coffee.

Glossary

acidity: in cupping and tasting, a reference to any sense of sparkle on the tongue. Can also refer to pH level in processing. See also pH.

acrylamide: a cancer-causing agent; a by-product of roasting, but barely present in the cup.

antioxidants: cancer-fighting agents found in coffee drinks.

arabica: short form of *Coffea arabica*, the better of the two main species in cup quality. See also robusta.

aroma: in cupping, the smell of brewed coffee.

ATV: all-terrain vehicle.

bag: a standard unit, 60 kilos or about 132 pounds of green coffee. *Bag* is the basic unit used to measure production and consumption around the world.

basis point: 1 basis point is .01 percent. The term *basis point* is used in economics to make a change in value or quantity clear, as opposed to the different interpretations of percentage increase.

BBB: blood-brain barrier.

beneficio: Spanish for "wet mill." See also wet processing.

body: sense of fullness on the tongue. Also called "mouth feel."

broca: Spanish for the coffee berry borer, *Hypothenemus hampei.*

cappuccino: an espresso-based drink that traditionally has $^1\!/_3$ coffee, $^1\!/_3$ steamed milk, and $^1\!/_3$ foamed milk. A "dry cap" has more foamed and less steamed milk; a "wet cap" is the opposite.

C price: the price of green coffee per 100 pounds, although sometimes quoted in dollars per pound, on the ICE at the next delivery date. See also ICE.

C.A.F.E.: Starbucks' Coffee and Farmer Equity Practices.

C2C: Crop to Cup, a private company.

certification: for coffee, approval by a national or international organization as meeting certain standards. Examples are Fair Trade, organic, and Rainforest Alliance.

chaff: light brown and fluffy, the last bits of silverskin, which blows off during roasting. See also silverskin.

channeling: when water passes through only part of a dose of ground coffee, especially in an espresso machine.

coffee berry borer: see *broca*.

coffee leaf rust: the fungus *Hemileia vastatrix*, in Spanish *la roya*.

***conilon*:** the word used in Brazil for robusta.

CQI: Coffee Quality Institute.

crema: Italian for cream. In espresso, the light brown foam on top of the liquor. See also liquor.

cupping: the act of tasting coffee in a highly regulated manner to determine its basic characteristics and quality. Green coffee buyers cup coffee they might buy, and in the best roasteries, coffee is cupped after each initial roast, or even more often as roasts proceed.

ΔT: delta T, rate of rise of temperature during roasting.

densimetric tables: motorized tables that separate beans by size and quality, with slanted beds that shake dried coffee beans and move them down the slope; also called gravity separators.

diterpenes: oily substances in unfiltered coffee liquor, for example, cafestol. They may be good for cholesterol level.

dripper cone: a conical piece of glass, plastic, porcelain, or other material into which a filter is set, ground coffee is added, and hot water is poured on to make a beverage.

dry mill: the second major stage of processing for any coffee. Here coffee is further dried on patios. It is then stored as parchment coffee for a while before being milled (hulled) to become "green" coffee. See also parchment.

dry processing: a process in which harvested beans are not pulped right away but are allowed to dry for a while on a patio or in a mechanical dryer.

ESC: European Society of Cardiology.

extraction yield: the percentage of solids in ground coffee that is extracted in the liquor.

F1: a first-generation hybrid produced by crossing existing arabica varieties with forest plants from Ethiopia.

farm gate price: the actual amount farmers are paid for their coffee, that is, not FOB or the amount paid to a co-op or other intermediary organization. See also FOB.

fermentation: the breaking down, in the absence of oxygen (anaerobic process), of a substance into a simpler substance. For harvested coffee, the action of microorganisms upon mucilage and/or coffee beans in which the level of pH decreases (the acid level goes up).

fines: small particles of ground coffee, smaller than the desired grain size. Some fines almost inevitably result from grinding.

finish: in cupping and tasting, lingering flavors in the mouth.

FLO: Fairtrade International (Fairtrade Labelling Organizations International).

FNC: Federación Nacional de Cafeteros de Colombia (National Federation of Coffee Growers).

FOB: free on board; refers to the price of any product on a ship, ready to be exported, after all costs in a producing country have been paid.

fragrance: in cupping, the smell of ground coffee before water is poured onto it.

FT: Fair Trade. Fair Trade USA, formerly Transfair USA, has separated from FLO and has different requirements for certification.

FTO: Fair Trade Organic.

fungibility: the ability to substitute one coffee for another and still achieve the same taste as the original blend had.

CGA: chlorogenic acid.

genetic editing: using an organism's own genes, manipulated in a lab, to short-circuit or prevent entirely the expression of some characteristic.

GIS: global information system.

GMO: genetically modified organism; also called transgenic, since one or more genes from one species are inserted into the DNA of another species.

GPS: global positioning system.

green coffee: beans after milling (hulling), ready to be shipped if exported and ready to be roasted.

GSF: geospatial farming.

Haber-Bosch process: developed in Germany in 1913. Ammonia is synthesized from air, allowing the creation of the first synthetic fertilizers.

heterosis: hybrid plant vigor.

HF: heart failure.

ICE: the current name of the International Commodities Exchange, located in New York. Formerly known as New York Commodities Exchange or NYBOT.

ICO: International Coffee Organization, based in London.

IFOAM: International Federation of Organic Agriculture Movements.

IHCAFE: Instituto Hondureño del Café (Honduran Coffee Institute).

honey coffee: another term for semi-pulped naturals.

JAB: JAB Holdings, a privately held German company.

latte: Italian for milk. An espresso-based drink topped with steamed milk, preferably of the consistency of paint. There are really no rules for proportions, which can vary from 1:1 coffee to milk to 1:7.

lipids: fatty acids produced in roasting coffee.

liquor: any coffee drink with nothing added, for example, espresso with no milk or sugar.

macchiato: Italian, "marked" or "spotted," referring to espresso drinks with dots of whole milk dropped onto the crema (regardless of how some chains make this drink).

Maillard reactions: the act of browning food during cooking, or simply from exposure to air, as happens with apple slices left out. In roasting coffee, these reactions help lock in flavor.

manzana: in Latin America, a measure of land area. The size of a manzana varies widely from country to country; in Argentina it is one hectare, while in most of Latin America it is about 1.72 acres or 6,961 square meters.

monsooned: in India, green coffee that has been spread out so that monsoon rain and wind can sweep over it for several weeks.

mucilage: the sticky and slightly sweet, soft material between the skin of coffee fruit and the next protective layer, parchment. See also parchment.

naturals: dry processed coffee beans. Semi-pulped naturals are processed by removing the skins from the fruit, then allowing the beans, still coated in mucilage, to dry for a time before they are taken to a dry mill.

NEJM: *New England Journal of Medicine.*

neurasthenia: an ailment of the white American middle and upper classes from the Civil War to at least 1914. The word meant "enervation" and "lack of virility."

organic: in farming, crops grown without the use of most synthetic fertilizers, sprays, or soil amendments.

organolepsy: my made-up word for an intense sensory experience.

organoleptic: having to do with strong sensory impressions.

parchment: a paper-like protective layer below the mucilage and above the silverskin in coffee fruit. "Parchment coffee" refers to coffee stored at a dry mill before it is hulled (milled).

peaberry: one single rounded bean in a coffee cherry instead of two half beans, each with a flat side. Peaberries are usually the result of the failure of one embryo to develop.

pH: level of acidity or alkalinity in a substance. Pure water has a pH of 7, considered neutral, neither acid nor base. The lower the number, the higher the acidity; higher than 7 indicates the substance is a base.

portafilter: a handle with a perforated basket inserted into a small basin at one end. The basket is filled with ground coffee and the portafilter is hooked into an espresso machine, ready for water to be forced through the puck, as the ground coffee is now called.

pour-over: see dripper cone.

press pot: another term for French press.

PROMECAFE: Regional Cooperative Program for the Technological Development and Modernization of Coffee Cultivation.

quintal: in Latin America, supposedly 100 pounds. In fact, a quintal varies widely among countries.

recalcitrant: for coffee, indicating the necessity to keep seed banks in the form of actual plants growing in fields. "Recalcitrant" here means unable to store seeds in vitro or in dried form.

refractometer: a hand-held device with a small cavity into which drops of coffee are placed. The refractometer registers the percentage of solids dissolved in the liquor, giving the extraction yield.

reverse osmosis (R/O) filtration: a built-in system that removes many unwanted chemicals and elements, for instance, chlorine, from water.

ristretto: Italian for "restricted"; an espresso drink that is smaller and much stronger—that is, having a higher ratio of coffee to water—than a regular shot.

robusta: the industry term for *Coffea canephora*, the more durable and rougher species of coffee, used in commodity blends and instant. However, robusta does have its admirers. Robusta is called *conilon* in Brazil. See also arabica.

roya: Spanish for coffee leaf rust. See coffee leaf rust.

Q graders: holders of the Q rating from the Coffee Quality Institute. Highly trained cuppers.

SAN: Sustainable Agriculture Network.

SCA: Specialty Coffee Association, formed as a merger of the SCAA, Specialty Coffee Association of America, and the SCAE, Speciality [sic] Coffee Association of Europe.

SHB: Strictly Hard Bean, a designation for high-grown coffee in parts of Central America.

silverskin: the last protective layer inside the coffee fruit; silverskin directly covers the beans. See also chaff.

single serving portions: pods and capsules, for example, K cups and Nespresso.

soluble: another word for instant coffee.

sustainability: essentially, the practice of keeping agricultural or other land productive. Not taking more nutrients out of the soil than are put back in.

technified: coffee bred to grow in full sun. Also called sun-grown.

terroir: French for "region" or "locality." A somewhat mystical term in the wine and coffee industries, referring not only to the land but to the care farmers give to their crops.

TDS: total dissolved solids.

trigonelline: an alkaloid compound that contributes to coffee's flavor in the cup.

ulema: organized Muslim clergy in any area.

USDA: United States Department of Agriculture.

USDA FAS: the Foreign Agricultural Service of the U.S. Department of Agriculture.

vasoconstrictor: any substance which causes blood vessels to constrict, raising blood pressure slightly.

vermicomposting: using worms to break down material removed from around coffee beans and caffeine left in such material.

VOC: (1) Vereenigde Oost-Indische Compagnie, Dutch East India Company; (2) volatile organic compound.

wet mill: where the first stages in wet processing occur. Here the fruit is pulped and initial fermentation as well as some drying takes place. Called *beneficio* in Spanish.

WCR: World Coffee Research.

xenobiotics: foreign substances in the body not produced by the host organism itself.

Notes

CHAPTER 1. INTRODUCTION

1. This is according to the research group Wevio, for example. http://www.wevio .com/global-coffee-industry-facts-statistics-of-2014-2015/, accessed November 18, 2017.

2. Gallup News. http://news.gallup.com/poll/184388/americans-coffee-consump tion-steady-few-cut-back.aspx, accessed November 18, 2017.

CHAPTER 2. IN PRODUCING COUNTRIES

1. Jacques Avelino et al., "The Coffee Rust Crises in Colombia and Central America (2008–2013): Impacts, Plausible Causes and Proposed Solutions," *Food Security* 7, no. 2 (April 2015): 303–21.

2. The data are taken from a presentation by Miguel Antonio Medina, "Il Cumbre de Roya," Coffee Rust Summit, Guatemala 2016. I am indebted for this reference to Hanna Neuschwander. The countries mentioned are those covered by the organization Promecafé.

3. Information on WCR is from my notes taken during a visit to Flor Amarilla in August 2017 and from World Coffee Research (WCR), *El futuro del café. Reporte Anual 2016.*

4. https://varieties.worldcoffeeresearch.org/varieties/milenio, accessed June 4, 2017.

5. SCAA [Specialty Coffee Association of America], "White Paper: A Blueprint to End Hunger in the Coffee Lands," 2013, esp. pages 4 and 5.

6. CARE, "Finding Local Solutions for Food Insecurity in Guatemala and Honduras," April 2014, 4.

7. WCR, *El futuro del café*, 33–34.

8. Pablo Imbach et al., "Coupling of Pollination Services and Coffee Suitability under Climate Change," *Proceedings of the National Academy of Sciences of the United States of America* 114, no. 39 (August 10, 2017), http://www.pnas.org/content/114/39/10438 .abstract, accessed November 18, 2017.

9. J. Kellermann et al., "Ecological and Economic Services Provided by Birds on Jamaican Blue Mountain Coffee Farms," *Conservation Biology* 22, no. 5 (2008): 1177 and passim.

10. As calculated from H. A. M. van der Vossen, "A Critical Analysis of the Agronomic and Economic Sustainability of Organic Coffee Production," *Experimental Agriculture* 41 (2005): 450, who notes that productivity per land unit has risen as much as eight times since 1900, about half of which is due to the use of inorganic fertilizers and pesticides.

11. http://www.coffeehabitat.com/2010/01/organic-coffee/, accessed April 10, 2017. Full citations to the studies are given at this site.

12. The quote is from A. E. Lyngbæk, R. G. Muschler, and F. L. Sinclair, "Productivity and Profitability of Multistrata Organic versus Conventional Coffee Farms in Costa Rica," *Agroforestry Systems* 53, no. 2 (2001): 205. The cost of fertilizer is on page 207. But IFOAM claims it found that farmers "engaged in certified organic export production in East Africa were significantly more profitable in terms of net farm income earnings than those that engaged only in conventional production." "Productivity and Profitability of Organic Farming Systems in East Africa" (2013): vi, https://link.springer.com/article/ 10.1023/A:1013332722014, accessed April 3, 2017.

13. See, for example, Peter Laufer, *Organic: A Journalist's Quest to Discover the Truth behind Food Labeling* (Guilford, CT: Lyons Press, 2014).

14. See the data for labor time and costs on a large organic farm in Chiapas, Mexico, compared to time and cost on nearby conventional farms: L. Pulschen and H.-J. Lutzeyer, "Ecological and Economic Conditions of Organic Coffee Production in Latin America and Papua New Guinea," *Angewandte Botanik* 67 (1993): 206. Productivity per hectare was also considerably lower on the organic farm, Finca Irlanda.

15. Van der Vossen, "A Critical Analysis," 449. And see V. E. Méndez et al., "Effects of Fair Trade and Organic Certifications on Small-Scale Coffee Farmer Households in Central America and Mexico," *Renewable Agriculture and Food Systems* 25, no. 3 (September 2010): 236–51.

16. IFOAM, "Productivity and Profitability in East Africa," vi. The citations to the work of van der Vossen and others on lower productivity and income in Latin America

are mentioned on page 19, without criticism of their findings. Africa's different conditions are given on page 21.

17. http://www.organic.org/home/faq, accessed May 11, 2017.

18. See the data for labor time and costs on a large organic farm in Chiapas, Mexico, compared to time and cost on nearby conventional farms: Pulschen and Lutzeyer, "Ecological and Economic Conditions," 204–8.

19. USDA, "Sustainable Agriculture: Definitions and Terms," compiled by Mary V. Gold, Special Reference Briefs Series no. SRB 99-02, Updates SRB 94-05, September 1999; revised August 2007, https://www.nal.usda.gov/afsic/sustainable-agriculture-definitions-and-terms#toc2, accessed April 17, 2017.

20. http://www.omafra.gov.on.ca/english/food/foodsafety/producers/gap-defini tions.ht, accessed April 17, 2017.

21. https://legacy.sweetmarias.com/library/node/5068, accessed October 26, 2017.

22. https://coopcoffees.coop/chajul/, accessed October 26, 2017.

23. *The Atlantic*, May 21, 2013.

24. Christophe Montagnon, "Coffee Production Costs and Farm Profitability: Strategic Literature Review," sponsored by the Specialty Coffee Association, October 2017.

25. All figures are from United States Department of Agriculture, Foreign Agricultural Service (USDA FAS), "Coffee: World Markets and Trade," June 2017.

26. I have based this section on Kelly Stein, "Unprecedented Precision: Advances in Geospatial Coffee Farming Conserve Water, Maximize Yield, and Can Reduce Production Costs as Much as 30%," *STIR*, no. 6 (2015): 32–34.

27. B. Rodriguez and M. Vasquez, "Economic Aspects of Coffee Production," in *Coffee: Growing, Processing, Sustainable Production*, ed. Jean Nicolas Wintgens (Hoboken, NJ: Wiley-VCH; 2nd edition, 2012): 833–35.

28. David Browning and Shirin Moayyad, "Ending Poverty," in *The Craft and Science of Coffee*, ed. Britta Folmer (Cambridge, MA: Academic Press, 2017), 109.

29. Root Capital Issue Brief Number 2, "Applying a Gender Lens to Agriculture: Farmers, Leaders, and Hidden Influencers in the Rural Economy," 2.

30. Quoted in Nick Brown, "The CQI [Coffee Quality Institute] Gender Initiative and Why Industry Should Care about Equity at Origin," Daily Coffee News by *Roast Magazine*, September 22, 2014, https://dailycoffeenews.com/2014/09/22/the -cqi-gender-initiative-and-why-industry-should-care-about-equity-at-origin/, accessed November 20, 2017.

31. Nicholas D. Kristof and Sheryl WuDunn, *Half the Sky: Turning Oppression into Opportunity for Women Worldwide* (New York: Random House, 2010).

32. https://www.coffeecan.org/our-work, accessed November 20, 2017.

33. https://www.coffeecan.org/our-work/peru, accessed November 20, 2017.

34. Root Capital Issue Brief Number 2, passim.

35. http://vegaalliance.org/coffee-quality-institute-partnership-for-gender-equity-gains-commitments-from-acdivoca-falcon-coffees-ltd-amfotek-and-mars-drinks/, accessed November 20, 2017.

36. CIA World Factbook, "Nicaragua," "People and Society" and "Economy" sections.

37. Catholic Relief Services, *Exploring Isolated Cases of Modern Slavery: Farmworker Protections and Labor Conditions in Brazil's Coffee Sector*, 2016.

38. Juan R. Sanz-Uribe et al., "Intestinal Fermentation," in Folmer, *Craft and Science*, 58–59.

39. Ibid., 63.

40. Nick Brown, Daily Coffee News by *Roast Magazine*, https://dailycoffeenews.com/2017/10/26/ninety-plus-panama-coffee-earns-2273-per-pound-described-as-evoking-erotic-innervation/, accessed November 1, 2017.

41. https://croptocup.wordpress.com/2011/07/12/financial-transparency-report-burundi-2010/, accessed December 1, 2017.

42. Oxfam, *Mugged: Poverty in Your Coffee Cup* (Oxford: Oxfam International, 2002), 26.

43. http://gcrmag.com/economics/view/the-cost-of-coffee-cultivation, accessed April 10, 2017.

44. "Coffee C® Futures," https://www.theice.com/products/15/Coffee-C-Futures, accessed April 21, 2017.

45. https://tradingeconomics.com/commodity/coffee, accessed October 12, 2017.

46. Multatuli (Eduard Dekker), *Max Havelaar: or the Coffee Auctions of the Dutch Trading Company*, trans. Roy Edwards (Leyden: Sijthoff, 1967), 74.

47. http://www.rainforest-alliance.org/articles/rainforest-alliance-certified-coffee, accessed May 1, 2017.

48. http://dailycoffeenews.com/2015/05/15/starbucks-claims-99-ethically-sourced-coffee-but-what-does-that-even-mean/.

49. https://www.starbucks.com/responsibility/community/farmer-support, accessed October 27, 2017.

50. One of the most thorough critiques of Fair Trade is by Colleen Haight, "The Problem with Fair Trade Coffee," *Stanford Social Innovation Review* (Summer 2011), https://ssir.org/articles/entry/the_problem_with_fair_trade_coffee, accessed May 2, 2017.

51. Jimmy Sherfey, "The Cost of Financially Sustainable Coffee Production," *Roast Magazine* (May/June 2017): 71–82.

52. This rating scale is common to the industry; it can be found at the Coffee Review site, http://www.coffeereview.com/interpret-coffee/, accessed November 1, 2017.

53. The Climate Institute, "A Brewing Storm: The Climate Change Risks to Coffee," September 2016.

54. http://old.grida.no/graphicslib/detail/impact-of-temperature-rise-on-robusta -coffee-in-uganda_64de, February 21, 2013, accessed June 5, 2017.

CHAPTER 3. ROASTING COFFEE, MAKING COFFEE DRINKS

1. http://www.sfchronicle.com/business/article/Class-opens-eyes-at-UC-Davis-to -coffee-as-a-field-9211532.php, September 28, 2016.

2. Roberto A. Ferdman, *Washington Post* Wonk Blog, February 24, 2015, https:// www.washingtonpost.com/news/wonk/wp/2015/02/24/its-true-americans-like-to-drink -bad-coffee/?utm_term=.53a2c9aeda33, accessed June 23, 2017.

3. Euromonitor International, "Coffee Report," October 2016.

4. Figures calculated by Brian Stoffel, February 28, 2015, using data from Euromonitor and the *Washington Post*, https://www.fool.com/investing/general/2015/02/28/ forget-starbucks-corporation-this-is-americas-bigg.aspx, accessed June 30, 2017. Stoffel is a widely published and cited writer for The Motley Fool.

5. https://www.statista.com/statistics/324659/jm-smucker-co-us-coffee-sales/, accessed June 22, 2017.

6. https://news.starbucks.com/news/q4-fy16-earnings, accessed June 23, 2016.

7. Jonathan Morris, "We Consumers—Tastes, Rituals, and Waves," in *The Craft and Science of Coffee*, ed. Britta Folmer (Cambridge, MA: Academic Press, 2017), 485.

8. https://www.starbucks.com/menu/drinks/espresso/pumpkin-spice-latte, accessed November 14, 2017.

9. https://www.huffingtonpost.com/grace-nasri/the-calories-in-your-coffee-_b_ 827427.html, accessed November 14, 2017.

10. https://www.statista.com/statistics/579810/costa-coffee-revenue/, accessed November 14, 2017.

11. *Washington Post,* February 24, 2015.

12. https://www.packagedfacts.com/Single-Cup-Brew-9422187/, accessed June 22, 2017.

13. *The Telegraph*, September 6, 2016, citing a report by Kantar Worldpanel.

14. *Washington Post*, March 5, 2015.

15. *New York Times*, February 7, 2012.

16. Statista 2015, quoted in Catherine M. Tucker, *Coffee Culture: Local Experiences, Global Connections*, 2nd ed. (New York: Routledge, 2017), 4.

17. See many *New Yorker* Starbucks and other coffee cartoons at https://www.google .com/search?q=New+Yorker+Starbucks+cartoons&rlz=1C1JZAP_enUS690US690&tbm =isch&tbo=u&source=univ&sa=X&ved=0ahUKEwjV2Pv_—XUAhWIWCYKHW5LAlk QsAQIOg&biw=1680&bih=944#imgrc=7xH0Tp1N0CBXMM, accessed June 30, 2017.

18. https://www.pinterest.com/pin/236790892880499147/, accessed June 30, 2017.

19. *The Onion* 33, no. 20, June 27, 1998.

20. https://www.statista.com/statistics/196590/total-number-of-snack-and-coffee -shops-in-the-us-since-2002/, accessed June 6, 2017.

21. Statista, "Number of International and United States Starbucks Stores from 2005 to 2016," https://www.statista.com/statistics/218366/number-of-international-and-us -starbucks-stores/, accessed September 4, 2017.

22. Avery Gilbert, *What the Nose Knows: The Science of Scent in Everyday Life* (New York: Crown, 2008), 6–10.

23. Ibid., 23–24.

24. See, for instance, David McRaney, "'You Are Not So Smart': Why We Can't Tell Good Wine from Bad," *The Atlantic*, October 28, 2011.

25. From a review of a Guatemalan coffee by Tom Thompson and colleagues at Sweet Maria's Coffee, quoted in William Ristenpart and Tonya Kuhl, *The Design of Coffee: An Engineering Approach*, 2nd ed. (Davis, CA: Ristenpart/Kuhl Publishing, 2016), 17.

26. "Ninety Plus Panama Coffee Earns $2,273 per Pound, Described as Evoking 'Erotic Innervation'," Daily Coffee News, https://dailycoffeenews.com/2017/10/26/ ninety-plus-panama-coffee-earns-2273-per-pound-described-as-evoking-erotic-inner vation/, October 26, 2017.

27. World Coffee Research, "Sensory Lexicon," version 2.0, 2017.

28. http://sprudge.com/denver-post-official-coffee-riding-fourth-wave-51898.html, February 3, 2014, accessed December 3, 2017.

29. United States Department of Agriculture, Foreign Agricultural Service (USDA FAS), "Coffee: World Markets and Trade," June 2017

30. "The Bean Belt Revisited," *Roast Magazine*, November/December 2017, 49.

31. Roberto A. Ferdman, "Here Are the Countries That Drink the Most Coffee— The U.S. Isn't in the Top 10," *The Atlantic*, January 15, 2014.

32. The information, which is easy to follow, can be found on the interactive map at http://www.ico.org/profiles_e.asp, accessed June 30, 2017. For re-exports, see the ICO paper "Re-exports of Coffee," September 20, 2012.

33. https://www.wineinstitute.org/resources/statistics/article86, accessed July 19, 2017.

34. http://www.scaa.org/?page=resources&d=facts-and-figures, accessed July 19, 2017.

35. Pierre Bourdieu, *Distinction: A Social Critique of the Judgement of Taste*, trans. Richard Nice (Cambridge, MA: Harvard University Press, 1984), 17.

36. Ibid., 6, 7, 35, 53–55, 70, 76, 231.

37. Wolfgang Schivelbusch, *Tastes of Paradise: A Social History of Spices, Stimulants, and Intoxicants*, trans. David Jacobson (New York: Vintage Books, 1993).

38. David Jacobson, in Schivelbusch, *Tastes of Paradise*, xiii note.

39. *Spectator* no. 412, June 23, 1712, 3:541. See also *The Tatler*, no. 108, December 17, 1709, 2:155.

40. Timothy Morton, *The Poetics of Spice: Romantic Consumerism and the Exotic* (London: Cambridge University Press: 2000), 55 and 33.

41. Ibid., 8–10.

42. Schivelbusch, *Tastes of Paradise*, 7.

43. Brian Cowan, *The Social Life of Coffee: The Emergence of the British Coffeehouse* (New Haven: Yale University Press, 2005), 11.

44. Ibid., 14.

45. My translation from the French in Monique Lansard, "Der Kaffee in Frankreich im 17. und 18. Jahrhundert: Modeerscheinung oder Institution?" in *Kaffee im Spiegel europäischer Trinksitten/Coffee in the Context of European Drinking Habits*, ed. D. U. Ball (Zurich: Johann Jacobs Museum, 1991), 127.

46. Michel Tuchscherer, "Coffee in the Red Sea Area from the Sixteenth to the Nineteenth Century," in *The Global Coffee Economy in Africa, Asia, and Latin America 1500–1989*, ed. William Gervase Clarence-Smith and Steven Topik (Cambridge: Cambridge University Press, 2003), 51.

47. Ralph S. Hattox, *Coffee and Coffeehouses: The Origins of a Social Beverage in the Medieval Near East* (Seattle: University of Washington Press, 1985). The first quotation is on page 11, the second on page 23.

48. Ulla Heise, *Coffee and Coffeehouses*, trans. Paul Roper (West Chester, PA: Schiffer, 1987), 12–14.

49. Leonhard Rauwolf, *Aigentliche Beschreibung der Raisz, so er vor dieser zeit gegen Auffgang inn die Morgenländer* (Laugingen: Verlag Georgen Willers getruckt durch Leonhart Reinmichel, 1582).

50. Helene Desmet-Gregoire, "Die Ausbreitung des Kaffees bei den Gesellschaften der Vorderen Orients und des Mittelmeerraums: Ubernahme and Herstellung von Gegenstanden, Anpassung der Sitten," in Ball, *Kaffee im Spiegel*, 109.

51. William Ukers, *All about Coffee*, 2nd ed. (New York: Tea and Coffee Trade Journal Company, 1935), 50.

52. Markman Ellis, *The Coffee House: A Cultural History* (London: Weidenfeld and Nicolson, 2004), 26–36. Ellis finds the claim that a coffeehouse existed in Oxford by

1650 to be unsupported by solid evidence. But Cowan, *Social Life of Coffee*, 90, says that a house did exist by then in Oxford.

53. Mark Pendergrast says there were more than 2,000 by 1700. Pendergrast, *Uncommon Grounds: The History of Coffee and How It Transformed Our World* (New York: Basic Books, 1999), 13.

54. Ukers, *All about Coffee*, 103–4 and 112.

55. Anthony Clayton, *London's Coffee Houses: A Stimulating Story* (London: Historical Publications, 2003), 16.

56. Felipe Ferré, *L'aventure du café* (Paris: Denoël, 1988), 189.

57. The lyrics, in German and English, are at http://www.bach-cantatas.com/Texts/BWV211-Eng3P.htm, accessed October 16, 2017.

58. Cowan, *Social Life of Coffee*, 76.

59. Roman Sandgruber, "Kaffeesuppe und 'kleiner Brauner,' Sozialgeschichte des Kaffeekonsums in Österreich," in Ball, *Kaffee im Spiegel*, 54.

60. Ibid., 62.

61. Clayton, *London's Coffee Houses*, 109.

62. See, for example, B. Ann Tlusty, *Bacchus and Civic Order: The Culture of Drink in Early Modern Germany* (Charlottesville: University of Virginia Press, 2001).

63. Ellis, *Coffee House*, 209.

64. Morton, *Poetics of Spice*, 25.

65. Scott Rao, *The Coffee Roaster's Companion* (self-pub., 2014), 1.

66. Shawn Steiman, *The Little Coffee Know-It-All: A Miscellany for Growing, Roasting, and Brewing, Uncompromising and Unapologetic* (Quarry Books), Kindle, locations 1509–1510.

67. Rao, *Companion*, 42–48.

68. Stefan Schenker and Trish Rothgeb, "Volume Increase and Structural Changes," in Folmer, *Craft and Science of Coffee*, 247.

69. Steiman, *Know-It-All*, location 706.

70. Chris Kornman, "The Relationship between Water Activity and the Maillard Reaction in Roasting," Daily Coffee News by *Roast Magazine*, November 22, 2017.

71. I have drawn heavily for the following description of extraction from "Coffee Extraction and How to Taste It," *Barista Hustle*, February 1, 2015, at https://baristahustle.com/, accessed October 5, 2017.

CHAPTER 4. COFFEE AND HEALTH, SOCIAL AND PERSONAL

1. Ralph S. Hattox, *Coffee and Coffeehouses: The Origins of a Social Beverage in the Medieval Near East* (Seattle: University of Washington Press, 1985), 3.

2. https://www.vitacup.com/pages/our-story, accessed November 30, 2017.

3. "Do You Need to Take Vitamins?" *Healthline* newsletter, n.d., https://www.health line.com/health/do-you-need-take-vitamins#overview1, accessed September 28, 2017.

4. Joseph A. Rivera, "Turning Up the Heat on Acrylamide," in Emily Puro, ed., *The Book of Roast* (Portland, OR: *Roast* magazine, 2017), 187.

5. https://buy.vitacup.com/vitamin-infused-coffee, accessed September 26, 2017.

6. Hattox, *Coffee and Coffeehouses*, 34–37. And see Eric Geoffroy, "La diffusion du café au Proche-Orient arabe par l'intermédiare des soufis: Mythe et réalité," in *Le commerce du café avant l'ère des plantations coloniales: Espaces, réseaux, sociétés (XVe–XIXe siècles)*, ed. Michel Tuchscherer (Cairo: Institut Francais d'archaeologie orientale, Cahier des annales islamologiques 20, 2001), 11.

7. Abdul-Karim Rafeq, "The Socioeconomic and Political Implications of the Introduction of Coffee into Syria, 16th–18th Centuries," in Tuchscherer, *Commerce du café*, 129.

8. Tuchscherer, "Commerce et production," in Tuchscherer, *Commerce du café*, 51.

9. Geoffroy, "Diffusion du café," in Tuchscherer, *Commerce du café*, 13.

10. For the "repugnant" idea, see Rafeq, "Socioeconomic and Political Implications," 127. Alan S. Kaye provides an example of the verb "to make dull" associated with hunger in "The Etymology of 'Coffee': The Dark Brew," *Journal of the American Oriental Society* 106, no. 3 (July–September 1986): 557–58.

11. Kaye, "The Etymology of 'Coffee.'"

12. Rafeq, "Socioeconomic and Political Implications," 129.

13. Hattox, *Coffee and Coffeehouses*, 40–41.

14. Quoted in ibid., 60.

15. https://ich.unesco.org/en/RL/arabic-coffee-a-symbol-of-generosity-01074, accessed October 10, 2017.

16. E. J. Clery, *The Feminization Debate in Eighteenth-Century England: Literature, Commerce and Luxury* (Houndmills, Basingstoke, UK: Palgrave Macmillan, 2004), 5, 19.

17. Cited in ibid., 43.

18. Ibid., 5, 19, 35, 43.

19. The pamphlet was *Crackfart & Tony; or the Knave and the Fool: in a Dialogue over a Dish of Coffee* (London?: 1680), 1, quoted in Steve Pincus, "'Coffee Politicians Does Create': Coffeehouses and Restoration Political Culture," *Journal of Modern History* 67 (December 1994): 807.

20. Jürgen Habermas, *The Structural Transformation of the Public Sphere*, trans. Thomas Burger with the assistance of Frederick Lawrence (Cambridge, MA: Harvard University Press, 1989), 27, 52, 32, 57. Habermas was concerned to show that the growth and popularity of coffeehouses in Britain had to do with emerging forms of

mercantile capitalism. That idea has been much debated and is well beyond the scope of this book.

21. Pincus, "'Coffee Politicians'," 811, 815.

22. The best discussion of these events is Brian Cowan, *The Social Life of Coffee: The Emergence of the British Coffeehouse* (New Haven: Yale University Press, 2005), 194–229.

23. Felipe Ferré, *L'aventure du café* (Paris: Denoël, 1988), 189.

24. Quoted in Robert Mantran, "Le café à Istanbul au xvii.e siècle," in *Le Café en Méditerranée: Histoire, anthropologie, économie. XVIIIe–XXe siècle*, ed. Paul Fabre (Aix-en-Provence: Institut de recherches et d'études sur le monde arabe et musulman, 1980), 9.

25. Ferré, *L'aventure du café*, 175.

26. Ibid., 190.

27. A useful treatment of the subject is William Doyle, *The Oxford History of the French Revolution*, 2nd ed. (Oxford: Oxford University Press, 2002).

28. I have based the detail in this section on conversations with people in Central America and on Jeffrey Paige, *Coffee and Power: Revolution and the Rise of Democracy in Central America* (Cambridge, MA: Harvard University Press, 1998), 13–15.

29. Figures are from the CIA World Factbook, https://www.cia.gov/library/publica tions/the-world-factbook/geos/nu.html, accessed October 16, 2017.

30. http://www.intracen.org/coffee-guide/world-coffee-trade/world-coffee-ex ports—-basic-figures/, accessed October 16, 2017.

31. Bryant Simon, *Everything but the Coffee: Learning about America from Starbucks* (Berkeley: University of California Press, 2009), 94–118.

32. Asaf Bar-Tura, "The Coffeehouse as a Public Sphere: Brewing Social Change," in *Coffee: Philosophy for Everyone: Grounds for Debate*, ed. Scott F. Parker and Michael W. Austin (Chichester, UK: Wiley Blackwell, 2011), 96.

33. Reproduced in William Ukers, *All about Coffee*, 2nd ed. (New York: Tea and Coffee Trade Journal Company, 1935), 50.

34. The "Petition" can be found in ibid., 470.

35. On John Harvey Kellogg, see Brian C. Wilson, *Dr. John Harvey Kellogg and the Religion of Biologic Living* (Bloomington: Indiana University Press, 2014).

36. An array of Postum ads can be found at https://www.google.com/search?q= Postum+ads&rlz=1C1JZAP_enUS690US690&tbm=isch&tbo=u&source=univ&sa=X &ved=0ahUKEwiI4eaGxsPXAhVD7oMKHZ4RBjkQsAQIJw&biw=1680&bih=933# imgrc=Q4uJqA6XC0jO_M, accessed November 16, 2017.

37. From Roundtable Report, "The Good Things in Life: Coffee as Part of a Healthy Diet and Lifestyle," Coffee and Health, from the Institute for Scientific Information on Coffee, September 2015, 4.

38. Neal D. Freedman et al., "Association of Coffee Drinking with Total and Cause-Specific Mortality," *New England Journal of Medicine*, 366: May 17, 2012, 1891–1904.

39. Ibid., 1904.

40. https://www.hsph.harvard.edu/nutritionsource/2015/02/23/ask-the-expert-coffee-and-health-2/, accessed October 17, 2017.

41. Masood Sadiq Butt and M. Tauseef Sultan, "Coffee and Its Consumption: Benefits and Risks," *Critical Reviews in Food Science and Nutrition* 51, no. 4 (2011): 368, 370.

42. Shalini Dixit et al., "Effects of Habitual Coffee Consumption on Cardiometabolic Disease, Cardiovascular Health, and All Cause Mortality," *Journal of the American Heart Association* 5 (2016).

43. "Latest Research Highlights Role of Coffee Consumption in Prevention of Parkinson's Disease," Coffee and Health, from the Institute for Scientific Information on Coffee and Health, 2017, citing four studies.

44. "Higher Coffee Consumption Associated with Lower Risk of Early Death," *Science Daily*, August 17, 2017, https://www.sciencedaily.com/releases/2017/08/1708 27101750.htm, accessed October 17, 2017.

45. Tom M. McLellan, John A. Caldwell, and Harris R. Lieberman, "A Review of Caffeine's Effects on Cognitive, Physical and Occupational Performance," *Neuroscience and Biobehavioral Reviews* 71 (December 2016): 294–312. Not paginated in the electronic version, http://www.sciencedirect.com/science/article/pii/S0149763416300690, accessed October 19, 2017.

46. http://www.webmd.com/vitamins-supplements/ingredientmono-979-caffeine.aspx?activeingredientid=979, accessed September 26, 2017.

47. N. J. Abbott, "Astrocyte-Endothelial Interactions and Blood-Brain Barrier Permeability," *Journal of Anatomy* 6 (June 2002): 629–38, https://www.ncbi.nlm.nih.gov/pubmed/12162730, accessed October 30, 2017.

48. Stephen Braun, *Buzz: The Science and Lore of Alcohol and Caffeine* (New York: Penguin, 1996), 130.

49. Joseph Stromberg, "This Is How Your Brain Becomes Addicted to Caffeine," Smithsonian.com, August 9, 2013, https://www.smithsonianmag.com/science-nature/this-is-how-your-brain-becomes-addicted-to-caffeine-26861037/, accessed October 14, 2017.

50. M. A. Addicott et al., "The Effect of Daily Caffeine Use on Cerebral Blood Flow: How Much Caffeine Can We Tolerate?" US National Library of Medicine, National Institutes of Health, October 30, 2009, https://www.ncbi.nlm.nih.gov/pmc/articles/PMC2748160/, accessed November 30, 2017.

51. Braun, *Buzz*, 149.

52. Ibid., 120.

53. Addicott et al., "Effect of Daily Caffeine Use."

54. Ibid.

55. Mayo Clinic Staff, "Caffeine Content for Coffee, Tea, Soda and More," http://www.mayoclinic.org/healthy-lifestyle/nutrition-and-healthy-eating/in-depth/caffeine/art-20049372, accessed September 29, 2017.

56. Rachel R. McCusker et al., "Caffeine Content of Decaffeinated Coffee," *Journal of Analytical Toxicology* 30, no. 8 (1 October 2006): 611.

57. http://thecoffeefaq.com/7health.html#caffeineindecaf, accessed September 29, 2017.

58. https://www.coffeechemistry.com/chemistry/alkaloids/caffeine-in-coffee, accessed December 5, 2017.

59. *Oxford English Dictionary*, s.v. "addiction."

60. *Harvard Health Letter*, January 2012, 5.

61. Ibid.

62. Miroslav Mišíka et al., "Impact of Paper Filtered Coffee on Oxidative DNA-Damage: Results of a Clinical Trial," *Mutation Research/Fundamental and Molecular Mechanisms of Mutagenesis* 692, nos. 1–2 (October 13, 2010): 41.

63. Stephanie Pappas, "Coffee May Protect against Some Skin Cancers," January 20, 2015, https://www.livescience.com/49500-coffee-melanoma.html, accessed October 19, 2017.

64. "Coffee Consumption May Decrease Stroke Risk," according to a study presented at the American Heart Association's Scientific Sessions, November 16, 2017. Findings were presented by Laura Stevens, University of Colorado in Aurora. http://www.neurologyadvisor.com/stroke/coffee-consumption-decrease-stroke-risk/article/707122/?DCMP=ILC-NEURO_Promo_20171125&cpn=&hmSubId=&hmEmail=N7gnLg8BX1w2tgg5JGRyWA2&NID=1437245644&dl=0&utm_source=newsletter&utm_medium=email&utm_campaign=na-promo-mailing-112517&spMailingID=18545531&spUserID=MTgxMDk3ODE5NTg5S0&spJobID=1142208602&spReportId=MTE0MjIwODYwMgS2, accessed November 30, 2017.

65. "Acrylamide Questions and Answers," U.S. Food and Drug Administration, https://www.fda.gov/Food/FoodborneIllnessContaminants/ChemicalContaminants/ucm053569.htm, accessed October 20, 2017.

66. Robert F. Nelson, "A Label Undeserved: [California's] Proposition 65 and Coffee," *Roast Magazine* (January/February 2011).

67. Mandreep K. Virk-Baker et al., "Dietary Acrylamide and Human Cancer: A Systematic Review of Literature," *Nutrition and Cancer* 66, no. 5 (2014), 775.

68. "Acrylamide in Coffee: Should You Be Concerned?" *Healthline Newsletter*, citing several studies, 2017. https://www.healthline.com/nutrition/acrylamide-incoffee#section1, accessed October 20, 2017. This statement is based on a paper writ-

ten by a panel headed by Diane Benford, "Scientific Opinion on acrylamide in food," EFSA [European Food Safety Authority] Journal, first published June 4, 2015. "The Panel concluded that the current levels of dietary exposure to AA are not of concern with respect to non-neoplastic [appearance of malignant or benign tumors] effects" in humans. However, the panel did note that animal studies show a link to tumors, which is a cause for concern.

69. L. A. Mucci and K. M. Wilson, "Acrylamide Intake through Diet and Human Cancer Risk," *Journal of Agriculture and Food Chemistry*, Epub July 15, 2008, https://www.ncbi.nlm.nih.gov/pubmed/18624443, accessed October 20, 2017.

70. "Acrylamide in Coffee: Should You Be Concerned?" *Healthline Newsletter*, citing several studies, 2017, https://www.healthline.com/nutrition/acrylamide-in-coffee#section1, accessed October 20, 2017.

71. Ryan F. LeBoeuf et al., "Evaluation of Exposures and Respiratory Health at a Coffee Roasting and Packaging Facility," U.S. Department of Health and Human Services Centers for Disease Control and Prevention, Report No. 2015-0082-3287, August 2017.

72. *Harvard Health Letter*, January 2012, 5.

73. http://www.coffeeandhealth.org/topic-overview/coffee-composition-nutritional-information/, Institute for Scientific Information on Coffee, 2017, accessed October 17, 2017.

CHAPTER 5. CONCLUSION

1. "The Bean Belt Revisited: The Future of Coffee," *Roast Magazine*, (November/December 2017): 54. The remarks came, in order, from Kim Elena Ionescu, SCA; Darrin Daniel, Alliance for Coffee Excellence; David Roche, Coffee Quality Institute; Roberto Velez Vallejo, FNC; Jennifer Gallegos, Farmer Brothers Inc. and International Women's Coffee Alliance; and Timothy Schilling, WCR.

Index

About the Author

Robert W. Thurston is the senior editor and contributor to the award-winning book *Coffee: A Comprehensive Guide to the Bean, the Beverage, and the Industry*. He has published widely in coffee trade magazines. On visits to farms and research stations in nine countries, he has talked with many landowners, managers, co-op officials, pickers, and other workers in the coffee industry. A frequent speaker on coffee, he has given talks on its history, problems, and prospects around the United States and internationally. He has also been managing partner of Oxford Coffee Company since 2012.

In a previous career, he earned a PhD in modern Russian history from the University of Michigan and taught at several universities for more than twenty-five years. His earlier publications explore the history of twentieth-century Russia and the USSR, the witch hunts in Europe and Salem, World War II, and lynching around the world. He is emeritus professor of history at Miami University.